The Films *of* Carole Lombard

The Films of
Carole Lombard

by FREDERICK W. OTT

THE CITADEL PRESS
Secaucus, New Jersey

Fourth paperbound printing

Copyright ©1972 by Frederick W. Ott
All rights reserved
Published by Citadel Press, Inc.
A subsidiary of Lyle Stuart, Inc.
120 Enterprise Ave., Secaucus, N. J. 07094
In Canada: George J. McLeod Limited
73 Bathurst St., Toronto 2B, Ontario
Manufactured in the United States of America
by Halliday Lithograph Corp., West Hanover, Mass.
Designed by William Meinhardt
Library of Congress catalog card number: 78-147831
ISBN 0-8065-0278-9

Acknowledgments

Grateful acknowledgment is extended to Frederick C. Peters and Mrs. Jean Garceau, who made many helpful suggestions during the preparation of the biographical section. Mr. Peters and Mrs. Garceau also lent a number of important photographs which have been included in the publication.

I must also express a debt of gratitude to the following persons: Donald Deschner; Ted Tetzlaff; Virgil Miller, A.S.C.; Roland Gross, A.S.C.; William H. Crain; Lynwood Dunn; and Gerard Notzon. I owe a special thanks to DeWitt Bodeen and the fine staff at the Library of the Academy of Motion Picture Arts and Sciences.

I have consulted research materials in a number of libraries: The Academy of Motion Picture Arts and Sciences; The Harold Leonard Collection in the Powell Library, University of California, Los Angeles; The Los Angeles County Public Library (Art Department); The Hobilitzella Theatre Arts Library, University of Texas; The British Film Institute, London; The Museum of Modern Art Film Library; and The Franklin D. Roosevelt Library, Hyde Park. The Directors Guild of America and the Screen Actors Guild were most cooperative in giving assistance.

Photographs and illustrated materials were obtained from the following sources: The Academy of Motion Picture Arts and Sciences; The British Film Institute; The Larry Edmunds Book Store; Collectors Book Store; Kenneth G. Lawrence; Bruco Enterprises; Oliver Dernberger; Gunnard Nelson; Chester Nelson; The Scroungers; and John Hampton.

I would also like to thank Mrs. Lucy Kluckhohn for typing the manuscript.   F.W.O.

Contents

Introduction

by Charles Champlin

To think about Carole Lombard now, nearly thirty years after her death in a Nevada plane crash, is to be reminded again that the movies are unique among all the arts in the strange and often unsettling things they do to our perceptions of time and reality.

Old movies may fade, literally, but in a curious sense they never really die and they seldom really age. They preserve action eternally, so that their endlessly repeating events are always happening *now*, before our very eyes.

And so it is that watching yesterday's films, like those of the lady celebrated in this book, can be a profoundly affecting and even disturbing experience, because we are seeing them in a kind of multiple perspective. They are now, and yet were long ago, and were perhaps a distant day's make-believing about an even more distant day. We watch with a sad, keen awareness of what the Fates, savage or benign, have long since visited upon the handsome young players gesturing there before us on the screen. We are reminded of their mortality—and of our own—but we are reminded also of the special magic which the movies have bestowed upon them, enabling them to go on dazzling us, perky and vibrant and imperishable, in the days after tomorrow just as in the dimming days before yesterday.

The trickeries of time and film seem never so haunting to me as in the interrupted life of Carole Lombard. She would have been sixty-one as I write this, and would I daresay have remained a remarkably alluring adornment in our day. It was clear that her lithe figure and the superb face with those unforgettably sculpted cheekbones would have lent themselves to maturity with matchless grace. And it takes no great effort to imagine for her an age-defying, soul-deep romantic élan, infused now as then with a kind of intelligent sensuality.

I suppose it is true to say that she died at the peak of her beauty, powers and fame, yet it may be even truer to say that her greatest achievements were still to come. I say this not out of easy sentiment but from a feeling that, as prototypical of her time as she was, she was also well ahead of her time. She was all Woman and all Liberated, a third of a century before the ladies began to demand full and unfettered citizenship.

Introduction copyright 1970 by Charles Champlin.

In the beginning Miss Lombard was the perfect embodiment of the star myths of early Hollywood. Her life helped to define them— the tomboyish, star-struck, fiercely energetic and ambitious kid from the Midwest (Fort Wayne) come to Hollywood as a moppet, appearing in her first film at twelve and, thanks to the kindly assistance of a family friend, joining the Mack Sennett Studio.

Within a decade of her departure from Sennett, she had become the highest-paid female star in Hollywood, earning just under $500,000 a year—an astonishing sum in a day when a dollar meant three to five times what it means today. Sifting through the yellowed clippings about her, as I did not long ago, you feel you are reading footnotes to a myth: the breathlessly reported marriage to co-star William Powell, the honeymoon cruise to Honolulu, her illnesses, her jewels stolen, her arm mauled by a chimpanzee, rumors of divorce, Gable, a war bond tour to Indianapolis.

But from all the glamour queen trappings emerged something and someone rather different and quite unexpected—the sophisticated comedienne, witty and self-reliant, a man's woman who not only went hunting and fishing with Gable but seems to have adored it, a lady who (one suspected) achieved independence without toughness, romance without self-indulgence and fulfilment in marriage without the loss of her own identity and sense of achievement.

She was breathtakingly beautiful in a day which demanded plastic beauty of its heroes and heroines. What would, I think, have led her on to still greater stardom were the interior qualities, of wit and unaffected wordly wisdom, untrammelled spirits, honesty, directness, and her apparent awareness that freedom is not necessarily the same thing as being alone and that the truest freedom is within a secure love.

From the slapstick beginnings, Carole Lombard had been evolving in a more interesting and exciting way—so it seems now—than almost any other actress of her day. Like films themselves, she appeared to be moving into new and uncommon ground of sensibility and intelligence, and toward the highest comedy, which arises from the truest contemplation of the world's ways.

It becomes almost impossible to judge old movies with any detachment, because we seem to see them through a scrim of our private accretions of memory, association and our sense of our own frail transience. But the existing achievements of Carole Lombard look stunning to our most ruthless and unsentimental eye. And that we cannot know what her ultimate triumphs might have been is not least of the sorrows of that January night above the Nevada desert.

CHARLES CHAMPLIN
Los Angeles *Times.*

(Champlin is entertainment editor and principal film critic of the Los Angeles *Times.*)

There was a subtle change . . . in the approved type of femininity as represented in the department store advertisements and the shop window manikins. The new type of the early nineteen-thirties was alert-looking rather than bored-looking. She had a pert, uptilted nose and an agreeably intelligent expression; she appeared alive to what was going on about her, ready to make an effort to give the company a good time. She conveyed a sense of competence. This was the sort of girl who might be able to go out and get a job, help shoulder the family responsibilities when her father's or husband's income stopped . . . and who would look, not hard, demanding, difficult to move deeply, but piquantly pretty, gentle, amenable, thus restoring their shaken masculine pride.

Since Yesterday, The Nineteen-Thirties in America,
Frederick Lewis Allen (Bantam, 1961) p. 112.

The loss of credibility in former values, the breakdown of the smug-
ness and self confidence of the jazz era, the growing bewilderment
and dissatisfaction in a "crazy" world that does not make sense, has
been reflected in a revival of comedies of satire and self-ridicule . . .
epitomized perhaps, in the title of one of them: *Nothing Sacred*.
The Rise of the American Film,
Lewis Jacobs (Harcourt Brace, 1939) p. 535

I remember . . . feeling genuinely saddened when Carole Lombard died in a wartime plane crash. It was not that she had ever been an object of romantic reveried to me, or even that I knew very much about her personally. It was that something witty, madcap, tough, earnest and even noble had gone out of life, something I would always associate with the "thirties: the zany rich girl with a good heart . . . who could drink with the boys, everyone's hip older sister who brought a whiff of the Big World when she visited home. She was funny and she was fun, she had something more substantial than glamour and her name evokes a point of view that I still encounter in the women of my generation.

John Clellon Holmes,
A *Harper's* essay, December, 1965

The Biography of
Carole Lombard

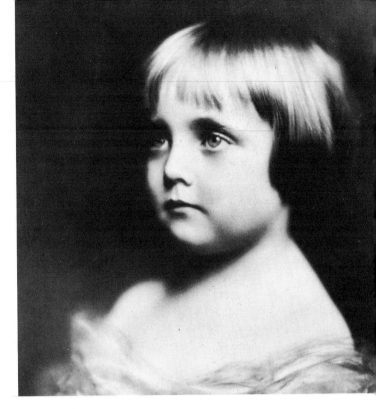

Jane Alice Peters.

Biography

Carole Lombard was born Jane Alice Peters on October 6, 1908, in Fort Wayne, Indiana, the daughter of Elizabeth Knight and Frederick C. Peters. Until the age of five, Jane Alice lived with her parents and two older brothers, Frederick and Stuart, in a comfortable frame bungalow on Rockhill Street in Fort Wayne. As a little girl, she was not very interested in "paper cutouts, making valentines or the usual pastimes of juveniles living in the West End neighborhood." An energetic youth, Jane rather "liked to tear out of her house . . . away from the maid's eye and proceed to the center parkway across the street and root for her brother's [Frederick Peters] winning baseball team." She enjoyed watching football, too, which the boys played in a triangular lot at the foot of Union Street. "In retrospect it was the Peters' little sister Jane who gave these sandlot games historical significance," remembered Robert Pollack, a childhood friend. "Every other afternoon this [five]-year-old blonde would come screeching across the street, demanding a chance to play one of the ends. She was always sent home again." Because there were few girls for Jane to play with on Rockhill Street, her brothers sometimes recruited her "for a cop-and-robber spree" with the neighborhood boys.

Her association with the boys during childhood and adolescence made Jane something of a "tomboy," but without destroying the feminine impulse. Perhaps this early association with the opposite sex deepened her understanding of the male mentality which, in later years, made her attractive to men who were to see in Lombard the ideal mate, a woman who could be as companionable as a pal. "If I have a masculine manner of thinking I am not sorry for it," she told an interviewer in the mid-1930's. "It has brought me fine friendships, and has made them last."

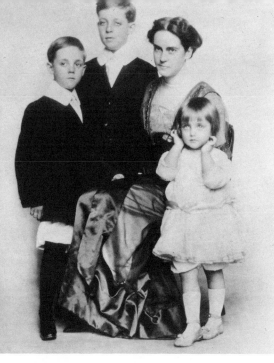

Stuart, Frederick, Mrs. Elizabeth Peters, and Jane Alice.

Jane Alice Peters in 1918, serving chocolate at a benefit in Los Angles for French orphans.

Jane Alice was introduced to the movies at the Colonial Theatre in Fort Wayne. On Friday nights, twice a month, the Peters family would attend the Colonial to see the latest chapter of the Kathlyn Williams serial, *The Adventures of Kathlyn*. The serial "dealt with the adventures of an American girl who, under compulsion, had inherited a throne in India and her problems therewith." On Saturday morning, to the amusement of her parents and brothers, Jane would give her own rendition of the latest episode, creating characters and dialogue that roughly corresponded to the celluloid adventures of the previous evening.

While attending Washington School in Fort Wayne, Jane may have appeared in her first theatrical, *The Talking Dog*. Later, when a group of neighborhood children produced *Ivanhoe* behind the home of Morgan Thieme, a playmate of the Peters', Jane Alice portrayed a handmaiden to Rebecca the Jewess. According to Pollack, who participated in this neighborhood drama, the children's "swords were lathe and our shields the tops of garbage cans. Court scenes were held in the Thieme barn and tourneys in the dirt alley." Lombard told an interviewer in 1936 that "upon another memorable occasion I was cast as Queen of the May. My brothers teased me to death, but I didn't mind too much. They let me wear a grand taffeta gown and a tiara, and that was compensation enough for the ragging."

Jane's Indiana childhood, the walks to Washington School on a snowy morning, the excitement of watching her brothers' team win at baseball, the dancing lessons at Mr. Trier's on Saturday afternoon, the occasional role in a neighborhood theatrical, and the pleasant summer holidays at Sylvan Lake near Rome City, ended in October, 1914, when her parents separated with Mrs. Peters and the children moving to California. "We planned to stay six months," Lombard recalled in 1932, "but luckily the climate lived up to even more than mother had hoped for and here we are, permanent fixtures." Elizabeth Peters, devoted to her children, established a home for the family in Los Angeles. In the years that followed, a particularly close relationship developed between Jane and her mother, "Bessie." Even at the height of her film career, Lombard remained in daily contact with "Bessie," her "staunchest friend and most inspiring benefactor." Adela Rogers St. Johns, who was acquainted with both Mrs. Peters and Lombard, wrote after their passing: "Someone said to me . . . that it seemed so awful that her mother should have been killed too. I can't feel that, knowing them. It would have been so awful for the one who was left."

While attending public schools in Los Angeles, Jane developed an interest in athletics. In junior high school she played volleyball regularly, mastered her tennis stroke, swam often, and received trophies for broad-jumping and running. She was never satisfied with amateur status in athletics, but strove to perfect her skill in whatever sport she tried. Practice in sports improved her coordination and timing and at a youthful age instilled a sense of fair play

Carole Lombard about 1925.

that friends and associates were to admire in the mature Carole Lombard.

At Virgil Elementary School Jane Alice Peters appeared as Mme. Darcourt in the play, *Pauvre Sylvie*. It is doubtful, however, that her appearance in the school play encouraged Al and Rita Kaufman, neighbors of the Peters, to persuade Allan Dwan, a pioneer motion picture director, to give her a small part in his film, *A Perfect Crime*. Jane Peters, a pretty girl of twelve with attractive blue eyes and blond curls, must have delighted Dwan who selected his film children with the greatest care. "There is nothing childlike about the vast majority of the children in moving picture plays," Dwan reported in a magazine article written in 1924. The director wrote that it was no easy task "to run out and pick for yourself a sweet and simple child, and then translate that sweet simplicity to the screen."

Dwan decided to feature Jane Peters in *A Perfect Crime,* a Fox film produced in 1921. For three days little Jane Alice impersonated the sister of Wally Griggs (Monte Blue), a bank clerk who leads a double life.

Jane completed her education at Virgil Junior High School. She never attended high school. The youthful and attractive Jane Alice Peters usually participated in exhibition ballroom dancing at the Coconut Grove in the Los Angeles Ambassador Hotel on Friday nights. On one such evening in 1925 an executive from Fox Pictures saw the attractive blonde dancing at the hotel and invited her to do a screen test at the studio. When the test proved successful, she was offered a contract to appear opposite Edmund Lowe in *Marriage in Transit,* a spy story directed by R. William Neill. Lowe played

With Edmund Goulding.

the dual role of conspirator and government agent, while Lombard took the part of the villain's girlfriend who marries the hero in the end. *Marriage in Transit* was not an outstanding film, but it seemed to please exhibitors who wrote favorably of Carole Lombard's performance in the role of Celia Hathaway.

Before the release of *Marriage in Transit* in March, 1925, Jane Peters adopted the screen name of Carole Lombard. Her new surname was borrowed from Mr. and Mrs. Harry Lombard whom her mother had met while serving in a soldiers' relief organization during World War I.

For her next Fox film she appeared opposite Charles "Buck" Jones in *Hearts and Spurs* directed by W. S. Van Dyke. Working with the talented Van Dyke appears to have been a pleasant experience for Lombard. One day while on location at the old Calico Mines near Barstow, California, Van Dyke and Jones conspired to play a practical joke on Lombard. On the previous day the naive, young actress had been told that Van Dyke became very angry when members of the cast appeared late on the set. The next day, she took particular care to be on the set ahead of schedule. Time passed, but where was Jones? When he finally arrived, Lombard watched nervously as Van Dyke confronted the tardy cowboy player. Then, suddenly, the director drew a pistol and fired at Jones who slumped to the ground. The actress looked on in horror as blood appeared to ooze from the "wounded" Jones. Having been asked to run to the river for water, she returned, only to find the director and Jones laughing hysterically. Astonished, Lombard emptied the contents of her pail on the two mirthmakers.

Lombard's next film for Fox was *Durant of the Band Lands,* again with Jones, released in November, 1925. She played only a small role, as the girlish Ellen Boyd whom the villains imprison in a mine shaft. Predictably, Jones secures her release at the crucial moment. "... They never would let me get in the fight," Lombard recalled of her appearances in the Fox westerns. "I had to simper at the hero and scream with terror when the heavy came after me. They never would let me get in there and give the villain a good

With her mother, Mrs. Elizabeth Knight Peters.

kick in the bustle." Her work at Fox appears to have ended with a small part in *The Road to Glory,* released in February, 1926. Directed by Howard Hawks, it told the "story of a speed-mad girl (May McAvoy) and the bitter road she followed before finding her real self and happiness."

In relegating Lombard to small roles, Fox may have been disappointed in her performance. When discussing this period in her career, Lombard admitted in an interview that although "Work before the camera was more fun than I had ever dared hope for in my most optimistic dreams . . . I did feel that I was sadly in need of experience." When the studio failed to renew its option on her contract at the end of the first year, Lombard seems to have remained off the screen until her move to Mack Sennett in 1927. It is very doubtful that the automobile accident with Harry Cooper, the son of a Los Angeles banker, seriously affected her film career. A splinter of a broken glass cut her cheek when another vehicle collided with Cooper's Bugatti roadster, but the wound healed properly, leaving an almost imperceptible scar which would not be difficult to disguise with makeup and proper lighting.

On the advice of Lonnie Dorsey, a family friend and an employee at Mack Sennett, Lombard made a screen test for the "King of Comedy." She passed the test and started to work at Sennett in early 1927, earning a salary of fifty dollars per week. If Carole Lombard was indeed conscious of her scar, as studio biographies and releases alleged in the 1930's, Sennett's camera promised her some protection. In photographing pretty girls, Sennett was more concerned with an attractive figure than a glamorous portrait view. "The face was used for two purposes," Mack Sennett recalled in 1930, "to hang funny moustaches on, and to be smeared with custard pie, plaster, flour, mud eggs or anything else the director could think of to have thrown." When a Sennett "script" required that Lombard paint her nose red, she good naturedly complied, not realizing that traces of the difficult-to-remove compound would remain for two weeks.

Mack Sennett remembered her as a "scamp and a madcap" much like Mabel [Normand]. Because her stay at the studio was comparatively short, Sennett "never got to know the girl very well." A reference to Lombard is contained, however, in the diary of Ruth Taylor for March 9, 1927: "On the last Sennett set I say there were ten new bathing girls. They looked eager and happy and beautiful. Mr. Sennett says Carole Lombard and Sally Eilers are the pick and they will be great stars some day."

At Sennett she appeared in a number of two-reel comedy shorts opposite Billy Gilbert, Chester Conklin, Daphne Pollard, Mack Swain, Dot Farley, Billy Bevan, Andy Clyde and Sally Eilers. A new Sennett comedy went into production approximately every Monday morning. Before work finished on Friday it was likely that Lombard had been spattered with custard pie, dumped into a horse trough or spanked with fence palings. "The theory was that if you could

Carole Lombard as she was to have appeared in DeMille's Dynamite.

With her eldest brother, Frederick Peters.

Lombard at the time of her marriage to William Powell, June 26, 1931. From left to right: Frederick Peters, Rosemary Zeiner, Stuart Peters, Lombard, and Powell.

'take it' there then you could do anything," Lombard recalled years later. Some of Carole Lombard's Sennett films for 1927 included: *Smith's Pony* and *The Girl From Everywhere*. In 1928 she made: *Run, Girl, Run, The Beach Club, The Best Man, The Swim Princess, The Bicycle Flirt, The Girl From Nowhere, His Unlucky Night, The Campus Carmen,* and *The Campus Vamp. Matchmaking Mamas* was released in 1929 after her departure from Sennett.

Lombard thoroughly enjoyed herself at Sennett. "There won't ever be another Sennett's for laughs," she told an interviewer in 1929. "Daphne Pollard and I were just in hysterics the whole time. We used to pull the worst gags on Matty Kemp and some of the boys over there. You should have seen that lot when the boys ran riot with water hoses—the mess we made off the set was often much worse than the one we did for the benefit of the cameras." Lombard recalled with characteristic good humor that it was Daphne Pollard "who was the real bathing girl because in every picture she made they turned the hose on her." She remembered Daphne as "the best sport of the whole gang. I remember when she and I got our final notices that the studio was going to close down. Well, that was the only time we were ever out of hysterics on that lot."

In his autobiography Mack Sennett made an overstatement when he claimed to have discovered Carole Lombard. Her experience at Sennett, however, was important in perfecting the fine comic sense that would distinguish her as a film comedienne in the period 1934 to 1942. Sennett was important to Carole Lombard,

With Clark Gable after the completion of
No Man of Her Own.

too, for another, more personal reason. On the Sennett lot she became acquainted with Madalynne Field, a fellow player, who as "Fieldsie" became Lombard's closest friend, secretary, and advisor.

In 1928, Lombard left Sennett to appear in *The Divine Sinner,* a Trem Carr Production distributed by Rayart. Directed by Scott Pembroke, this feature film appears to have been copyrighted and distributed under another title following its release in the summer of 1928. Lombard played a small role in the production that featured Vera Reynolds, Nigel DeBrulier, and Ernest Hilliard.

With the completion of *Divine Sinner,* Lombard moved to Pathé to appear in *Power* opposite William Boyd, Alan Hale, and Jacqueline Logan. Directed by Howard Higgins, *Power* was an inconsequential work made like a "two reel comedy...dragged to feature length."

Lombard appeared next in *Me, Gangster,* capably directed by Raoul Walsh and co-starring June Collyer and Don Terry. Based on a *Saturday Evening Post* story by Charles Francis Coe, it chronicled the life of a criminal, Jimmy Williams.

Having seen Lombard in a Sennett comedy, Paul Stein, a director at Pathé, offered her the role of "the other woman" in his production of *Show Folks.* Although the comedy sequences with Eddie Quillan were reviewed favorably, the film in general disappointed critics.

Under contract at Pathé, earning a salary of one hundred fifty dollars per week, Lombard appeared next in *Ned McCobb's*

With Clark Gable in No Man of Her Own, *the only motion picture in which they appeared together.*

With Clark Gable during the filming of No Man of Her Own.

Daughter, based on the play by Sidney Howard. The screen adaptation, directed by William J. Cowen, co-starred Irene Rich, Theodore Roberts, and Robert Armstrong.

In early 1929, Lombard was selected by Cecil B. DeMille to appear in *Dynamite* at Metro-Goldwyn-Mayer. The announcement of her casting was accompanied by a generous amount of publicity. Lombard was quoted in an interview as stating that she had discovered "the other side of C.B.'s majestic front" and was sure that "he's going to be great to work with." DeMille, however, changed his mind and dropped her from the production. Undaunted, Lombard continued her busy schedule at Pathé.

Howard Higgins directed Lombard in her first all-talking picture, *High Voltage,* from a story by Elliot Clawson. William Boyd, identified by a Pathé advertisement as representing the "clean, wholesome romance, and the buoyant optimism of America today," played the leading character. With Lombard cast as a sheriff's prisoner, the story focused on a group of people stranded in the High Sierras during a snow storm.

In *Big News,* skillfully directed by Gregory La Cava, Lombard played the wife of a newspaperman who is addicted to alcohol and the wisecrack. Critics seemed to enjoy the film; one reviewer ranked it "among [the] best newspaper stories filmed since sound arrived." Frank Reicher's humorous dialogue was a major contribution to the success of *Big News.* (Typical was Armstrong's reaction to the news that he has been fired from the paper: "There are 1,800 newspapers in the country and I have only worked on sixteen of them.")

Lombard appeared to enjoy her tenure at Pathé, which terminated with the completion of *The Racketeer,* again with Armstrong, in late 1929. The previous spring she had told an interviewer: "This is the studio where I just keep right on having hysterics the whole time—something approaching the way it was at Sennett's. Everyone's so darn pleasant. Do we get a lot of laughs? Well, I should say so. Today I just went on Von Stroheim's set and got myself introduced as if I were just a poor little girl trying to get along. Von didn't know me from Eve and he offered to give me a few days work as an East African tart—that is, if I looked the part well enough in one of the costumes they had. It was a riot." In a more serious vein, the apprentice actress had gained valuable experience at Pathé, working with outstanding directors like Howard Higgins, Raoul Walsh and Gregory La Cava. Lombard recalled in an interview in 1935: "We used to turn our hands to everything. We'd all get together on a story conference. If I had an idea I'd pop out with it, and whether it was accepted or not I was learning. I had a 'story' mind and found it helpful. In the easy camaraderie of a small studio we all had a hand in the pie."

Lombard returned to Fox in early 1930 to appear opposite Warner Baxter in *The Arizona Kid,* a sequel to *In Old Arizona.* Critics rightfully objected to the casting of Lombard as the villainous Virginia Hoyt.

Lombard's Paramount contract, negotiated in 1930, awarded her three hundred fifty dollars per week with a gradual increase to thirty-five hundred by 1936. Her first film for Paramount Pictures was *Safety in Numbers* opposite Charles "Buddy" Rogers. A weak scenario called for three chorus girls, Lombard, Kathryn Crawford and Josephine Dunn, to escort a young millionaire, played by Rogers, around New York. Predictably, all three fall in love with the crooning playboy who, in the end, declares his love for Miss Dunn.

Fast and Loose, Lombard's next release, was described as "a laugh and live drama of middle-aged conservatism versus youthful light-footedness." Lombard, described by a Paramount publicist as "probably one of the most widely known actresses through the medium of the fan magazines," co-starred with Miriam Hopkins, Frank Morgan and Henry Wadsworth. With the release of *Fast and Loose* in November, 1930, Paramount officially added the "e" to Carol in preparing her screen credits.

In 1931, Lombard appeared with Skeets Gallagher, Eugene Pallette and Norman Foster in an amusing comedy, *It Pays to Advertise*, directed by Frank Tuttle. Lombard was pert and attractive as the secretary who helps the son of a soap manufacturer to become his father's business rival.

Lombard starred next opposite her future husband, William Powell, in *Man of the World*. Under the direction of Richard Wallace and Edward Goodman, the Herman J. Mankiewicz screenplay cast Powell as an extortionist who falls in love with an American debutante (Lombard) whom he had intended to blackmail. Lombard and Powell appeared together again in *Ladies' Man*, directed by Lothar Mendes from a story by Rupert Hughes.

Carole Lombard, the ascending star had met William Powell, the older and more established player, in October, 1930. After an acquaintance of eight months they were married on June 26, 1931. The marriage ended in divorce twenty-eight months later on

*With her tennis instructor,
Elinor Tennet, in 1935.*

In the summer of 1935, Lombard hosted a party for A. C. Blumenthal and William Rhinelander Stuart at the Venice Pier Fun House, attended by almost the entire film colony. Seated with Lombard are Randolph Scott, Blumenthal, Stuart, Toby Wing, and Cary Grant.

With Claudette Colbert.

With Constance Talmadge at the Venice Pier party.

August 18, 1933. In an interview with Mark Dowling in 1936, Lombard stated that her "career had little to do with the divorce. We were just two completely incompatible people." Lombard and Powell, however, remained on friendly terms. In another interview she said: "I must like the man, or I wouldn't have married him in the first place! Now that we're divorced, we're still the best of friends." In 1936 they co-starred again in one of the brightest comedies of the decade, *My Man Godfrey.* Gregory La Cava, who directed *Godfrey,* remarked at the time how well they worked together, "like a congenial, loyal brother and sister."

Lombard's performance in *Up Pops the Devil,* a comedy about a married couple in Greenwich Village, delighted critics while her performance opposite Gary Cooper in *I Take This Woman,* directed by Marion Gering and Slavko Vorkapich, was received with less enthusiasm.

On the day following the release of *I Take This Woman,* Lombard and Powell departed on a honeymoon cruise to Hawaii. Returning to Los Angeles in the summer of 1931, she suffered an attack of pleurisy and did not resume film work until the fall. Her next vehicle was *No One Man,* co-starring Ricardo Cortez and Paul Lukas. The marital affairs of Penelope Newbold, a rich society girl, were unimaginatively presented in a cliché-ridden story directed by Lloyd Corrigan.

More disappointing, however, was *Sinners in the Sun,* co-starring Chester Morris, Adrienne Ames, Alison Skipworth, and Cary Grant. It wasted a good cast on a story "rather elderly in theme, and hardly distinctive in treatment." On loan to Columbia Pictures, Lombard appeared next in *Virtue,* the story of a street walker who mends her ways, and finally proves to her husband that she is deserving of his faith. The quick verbal exchanges between Mae (Lombard) and the wisecracking taxi driver (Pat O'Brien) made *Virtue* a moderate success.

Lombard remained at Columbia to make *No More Orchids,* directed by Walter Lang, the future husband of her closest friend, Madalynne Field. A distinguished cast included Walter Connally, Louise Closser Hale, Lyle Talbot and C. Aubrey Smith.

Returning to Paramount, Lombard appeared in her only film with Clark Gable, *No Man of Her Own,* directed by Wesley Ruggles from a screenplay by Maurice Watkins and Milton Gropper. As Connie Randall, a small-town librarian, Lombard reforms a crooked gambler, "Babe" Stewart, played by Gable.

Lombard's next film, *From Hell to Heaven* directed by Erle C. Kenton, recalled *Grand Hotel* and *If I Had a Million.* It studied the lives of various characters who gather at the Luray Springs Hotel to bet on a single race, the Capitol Handicap. *Supernatural,* released in the spring of 1933, created enough mystery and suspense to please some critics.

In *The Eagle and the Hawk,* a story from the First World War, Lombard appeared as "the beautiful woman" in a short scene with Fredric March. March, in the role of a dissolutioned aviator, attends a social affair in London. After listening to the officers boast of their achievements in battle, the young flyer leaves the party with a beautiful woman (Carole Lombard). Later, in the park, they sip champagne. Thinking of the warmongers he encountered at the party, March inquires, "Why can't they be kind?" With the utterance of her reply: *"I* want to be kind," the scene fades and Lombard's "beautiful woman" is never seen again.

Lombard accepting a portrait of herself from a silhouette artist at the Venice Pier.

With Mildred Evelyn Brook, Clive Brook, Warner Baxter, and Walter Wanger.

*With Fred MacMurray on the
set of* True Confession, *1937.*

On loan to Columbia, Lombard appeared in *Brief Moment*, directed by David Burton from a play by S. N. Behrman. Co-starring Gene Raymond and Arthur Hohl, *Brief Moment* was the first of ten Lombard films to be photographed by the gifted Ted Tetzlaff. Upon completion of *Brief Moment*, the cinematographer accepted Lombard's invitation to join her at Paramount. Tetzlaff made a careful study of Lombard's face. Noting its unusual contour—and discovering that it was not an easy task to photograph Carole Lombard's face—he carefully prepared the camera angle and lighting of each shot. Lombard encouraged Tetzlaff to give definition to her hollow cheeks, a quality which she admired in the facial structure of Marlene Dietrich.

Back at Paramount Lombard completed her 1933 production year with *White Woman*. In a tropical setting by Hans Drier and Harry Oliver, Lombard took the role of Judith Denning, a cynical but kind-hearted entertainer who is forced by circumstances to marry a cruel plantation boss, played by Charles Laughton.

Lombard appeared next in *Bolero*. Its most memorable scene was the dance to Ravel's *Bolero* which Lombard and George Raft performed atop a circular stage surrounded by native drummers in a lavish nightclub setting.

Before the completion of *Bolero*, Lombard started to work on *We're Not Dressing*, a musical version of the James M. Barrie play, *The Admirable Crichton*. Directed by Norman Taurog, Lombard appeared with Bing Crosby, Ethel Merman, George Burns, and Gracie Allen. While the Paramount company was filming on location at Catalina Island, Lombard appears to have been responsible for her usual number of practical jokes. In the film, however, Burns and Allen, Ethel Merman, and Leon Errol overshadowed her in comic situations. *We're Not Dressing* afforded many pleasant moments for general audiences and the growing legion of Crosby fans.

As *We're Not Dressing* neared completion, Lombard began work on *Twentieth Century* at Columbia Pictures. Based on the play by Ben Hecht and Charles MacArthur, the film contained a multitude of humorous situations involving an eccentric Broadway impresario, Oscar Jaffee, portrayed with consummate skill by John Barrymore, and his "hand-made star," Lily Garland, wonderfully played by Carole Lombard. Lily and Jaffee indulge in a fair amount of kicking and screaming, orchestrated by the opening and closing of compartment doors as the *Twentieth Century* races from Chicago to New York. Mixing sweetness with insult, Jaffee makes a feverish attempt to recruit Lily, "a woman in ten million, a creature apart," for the starring role in his production of the *Passion Play*. Before the *Limited* reaches New York, Jaffee, assisted by a nervous manager (Walter Connolly) and a fast-talking press agent (Roscoe Karns), has tricked Lily into signing a contract.

Director Howard Hawks appears to have selected Carole Lombard for *Twentieth Century*. Her performance during rehearsal, the first day, however, disappointed both Hawks and Barrymore. "She acted like a schoolgirl," Hawks recalled,

... and she was stiff, she would try and imagine a character and then act according to her imaginings instead of being herself.... John Barrymore began to hold his nose. I made him promise that he wouldn't say anything until three o'clock in the afternoon, but I could see him getting very worried over her stiffness, and obviously nothing was happening with this girl. Well, I took Lombard for a walk around the stage, and I said you've been working hard on the script. She said I'm glad it shows. And I said yes, you know every word of it. And I said how much do you get paid for the picture? She told me. I said that's pretty good. I said what do you get paid for? She said, well, acting. And I said well what if I would tell you that you had earned all your money and you don't owe a nickel, and you don't have to act anymore? And she just stared at me, and I said what would you do if a man said such a thing to you?

Lombard replied that she would kick anyone who said that, and when told that Barrymore had made the remark, she "smiled ... with one of those Lombard gestures." Hawks then told her that Barrymore would say that to her in the script. "Now," admonished the director,

> we're going back in and make this scene and you kick him, and you do any damn thing that comes into your mind that's natural, and quit acting. If you don't quit, I'm going to fire you this afternoon. You just be natural. And she said, are you serious? And I said I'm very serious. And she said all right. And we went back in and I said we're going to make this scene and Barrymore said oh, we're not ready. And I said who's running this? And he said, you are, okay. And we made about an eight page scene and she made a kick at him and he jumped back, and he started reacting and they went right through the scene. He made his exit, and I said cut and print it. And he came back in and he said to Lombard, that was marvelous, what've you been doing, kidding me? And she started to cry and ran off the stage. And he said, what happened? I said you've just seen a girl that's probably going to be a big star, and if we can just keep her from acting, we'll have a hell of a picture. And she became a star after the picture.

While at work on *Twentieth Century* Lombard told William Fleming that "doing a picture with Barrymore is wild and delicious. It is Experience with a capital 'E'. You start in as one person and emerge quite another. But you learn! Ah, what you learn.... It was he [Barrymore] who taught me to 'let go,' to abandon myself to my part.... It is the inherent self-consciousness of the normal individual that shackles his or her expression; that makes it difficult to throw one's self wholeheartedly and unreservedly to a part." John Barrymore's "terrific energy and absolute abandon got into your blood, and you forget your own fears and hampering re-

Motoring on the Selznick lot.

straints," she told Fleming. "He made me forget mine so completely that when, as Oscar Jaffee, the producer, he bellowed at Lily Garland, the actress, I found myself shrieking back at him. . . . When he threw out his arms and tore at his hair, I clutched my throat and 'hystericated'—forgetting everything except to live the character into which this wild producer was molding her. . . . In the rushes of *Twentieth Century* I have seen, I hardly recognize myself. I certainly am not the Carole Lombard of the past four years. . . ."

Carole Lombard had the highest professional regard for Barrymore, who had developed a great admiration for the young star. "I never dreamed Lombard had such a performance in her. Her work is superb. Her art in this picture is compelling, understanding and convincing," Barrymore told Fleming. "She has caught the mood of it, and gives to Lily Garland an unexpected degree of glamour and fascination. As Mildred Plotka, she is arresting, as Lily Garland, astounding." Lombard was particularly touched by Barrymore's gift of an autographed portrait bearing the inscription, "to the finest actress I have worked with, bar none." Barrymore's words had a special meaning for Carole Lombard. In 1935 she told an interviewer, "I knew that all those years of striving had brought me to my goal and that I had at last been accepted by the inner circle; that at last I could call myself [an] actress."

Lombard returned to Paramount to appear with Gary Cooper and Shirley Temple in *Now and Forever,* a film which retains its appeal after more than a quarter of a century. In the story of a swindler's love for his little daughter, Lombard was generally excellent as the crook's mistress and accomplice. Carole Lombard appeared next with Walter Connolly, Roger Pryor, and Arthur Hohl in *Lady By Choice,* a comedy, directed by David Burton for Columbia. On loan to MGM, Lombard trudged through a gangster yarn, *The Gay Bride,* opposite Chester Morris. Marion Gering's production of *Rumba* followed next. Released in 1935, it duplicated, with slight variation, the theme of *Bolero.* In this case, the ambitious dancer (George Raft), in love with a society woman (Lombard), is threatened with assassination on the night of his New York debut.

In *Hands Across the Table* Lombard revealed that fine comic sense which had distinguished her work in *Twentieth Century.* Directed by Mitchell Leisen from a scenario by Norman Krasna, *Hands Across the Table* is remembered as one of her finest films. Lombard played Regi Allen, a cynical manicurist, who wants to marry a wealthy husband, but falls in love with an impoverished playboy (Fred MacMurray).

In one unforgettable sequence, Regi and the playboy, Theodore Drew, conspire to dispose of a shy suitor who calls at her apartment with candy and flowers. Answering the door in his undershirt and shorts, Drew seizes the gifts intended for Regi; dumbfounded, the astonished visitor crosses the threshold. In the apartment Drew pretends to be Regi's cruel husband who has just returned home. "Palming herself off as single, uh?" he asks the man in a disgusted

"*Beau Brummel,*" *Carole Lombard's pet English sheep dog, on the set of* Made for Each Other. *Director John Cromwell and his assistant Eric Stacey look on.*

With her personal hairdresser,
Loretta Francell.

*Lombard displays a portfolio of her early photographs to James
Stewart and Donald Briggs during the filming of* Made for
Each Other.

tone. Ill at ease and not a little frightened, the suitor listens as Regi
and Drew, off camera, stage a mock battle in the bathroom. Drew's
angry voice is answered with an occasional remark from Regi, "I'll
tell my mother on you!" The hollering continues when Drew returns
to the livingroom, pretending to search for something. "Regi!" he
calls out, "what did you do with that *gun?*" With the utterance
of this last word the frightened suitor dashes out the front door as
Regi and Drew break into laughter. The scene is a marvelous
blend of dialogue and imagery.

Lombard appeared next opposite Preston Foster in *Love Before
Breakfast,* directed by Walter Lang for Universal. In *The Princess
Comes Across,* Lombard played a Brooklyn show girl who mas-
querades as a Swedish princess.

The Princess Comes Across was still in production when Lombard started to work at Universal in 1936 on *My Man Godfrey.*
Lombard was perfectly suited for the role of Irene Bullock. Her
fine performance, perhaps the greatest of her career, received a
most deserved Academy Award nomination. Directed by La Cava
and photographed by Tetzlaff, Lombard co-starred with William
Powell. Eugene Pallette, Alice Brady, Gail Patrick, Mischa Auer
and Alan Mowbray were outstanding in supporting roles. Audiences
everywhere seemed to respond enthusiastically to what was surely
the "daffiest comedy of the year." The film clearly established
Lombard as a comedienne of the first rank.

Returning to Paramount, Lombard appeared a little less "screwball" in the romantic comedy, *Swing High, Swing Low*. It was an outstanding film, superbly photographed by Tetzlaff in a studio Panama created with meticulous care by Hans Drier and Ernst Fegte.

With the completion of *Swing High, Swing Low*, Lombard started to work on her last Paramount film, *True Confession*, directed by Wesley Ruggles. Lombard played Helen Bartlett, a delightful "screwball," who finds it necessary to confess to a murder she did not commit. Believing his wife guilty, her husband (Mac-Murray) secures her acquittal after entering a plea of justifiable homicide in defense of chastity. John Barrymore, Una Merkel and Edgar Kennedy delivered outstanding performances in supporting roles.

Upon the expiration of her Paramount contract in 1937, Lombard signed an agreement with film producer David Selznick. Her first film for Selznick-International was a Technicolor production, *Nothing Sacred*, directed by William Wellman from a screenplay by Ben Hecht. Humorist Dorothy Parker enlivened the scenario with additional dialogue.

Gable and Lombard en route to Atlanta to attend the premiere of Gone With the Wind, *December, 1939.*

Nothing Sacred recounted the experiences of Hazel Flagg, a small town girl, who is cynically exploited by a New York newspaper when it is learned that she has only six months to live. Cook (Fredric March), a reporter on the paper, brings the "dying" girl to New York where "the little soldier whose heroic smile in the face of death" wrings "cheers and tears from the great stone heart of the city." The ballyhoo is without parallel: she is honored by the mayor and serenaded by school children; a waiter cries in the champagne while an airplane writes 'Hazel' in the sky. Eventually, however, her benefactors learn that the illness is a fraud. To protect Cook, whom she now loves, Hazel agrees to stage a mock suicide. Disguised in sunglasses, Hazel and the reporter sail away on an ocean liner while a day of mourning is proclaimed for her funeral.

Nothing Sacred proved to be a marvelous satire in its treatment of journalistic practices and the gullibility of the urban masses. It focused its attention, too, on the mentality of the small town, brilliantly represented by the storekeeper (Margaret Hamilton) who charges fifty cents for answering questions "Yep" or "Nope"; Doc Downer (Charles Winninger), the town physician who becomes the girl's accomplice; and the village beauty herself, Hazel Flagg, who cynically outwits the cynical press. Released at the close of 1937, *Nothing Sacred* elevated Lombard to the peak of stardom. It was difficult to deny Peter Galway's comment that she possessed "a touch of comic genius."

The triumph of *Nothing Sacred* was followed by the disaster of *Fools for Scandal*, produced and directed by Mervyn LeRoy for Warner Bros. *Fools for Scandal* suffered from a poor scenario, the work of Herbert and Joseph Fields who were assisted at some point by Irving Beecher. Distinguished by the absence of clever dialogue, the Fields-Beecher screenplay reworked the theme of *My Man Godfrey:* an impoverished nobleman (Ferdinand Gravet) becomes the butler in the household of a movie star (Lombard). Even the screen's most gifted comedienne could not redeem a property that was beyond redemption. When James Reid interviewed Lombard on the set of *Fools for Scandal,* it is not unlikely that the star had her current production in mind when she stated that comic roles were the most difficult because the actor must convince himself that what he is doing is funny. The actress reflected that "the only time it comes easy is when you're doing a scene that would be funny, no matter who played it." Critics wrote unfavorably of *Fools for Scandal,* Lombard's only film for Warner Bros. and her last picture to be photographed by Tetzlaff.

For over two years public attention had focused on the relationship between Carole Lombard and Clark Gable. Gable and Lombard had met in 1932 while co-starring in *No Man of Her Own.* Their romantic attachment, however, dated from February, 1936, when John Hay Whitney gave an elaborate costume party for Hollywood notables. The invitations requested that guests appear in something white. With her unfailing sense of humor, Lombard arrived at the party in a white ambulance and was carried into the Whitney mansion on a stretcher. At the "White Ball" Gable and Lombard renewed their friendship, becoming constant companions until their marriage in 1939.

Lombard and Gable cemented their relationship with an array of "gag" presents which made wonderful publicity. One Valentine's Day, Gable opened his garage door to find a Model T Ford decorated with red hearts; Gable reciprocated by sending Lombard an old fire engine. On another occasion, she presented him with a stuffed goat, elaborately gift wrapped. Another Lombard parcel addressed to Gable contained a ham with his portrait on the wrapper. *Parnell,* Gable's great screen failure, gave rise to a number of jokes. In 1939, Lombard ordered that hundreds of leaflets be printed with the words "Remember Parnell" for aerial distribution over the MGM lot in Culver City. She was restrained, however, by a studio executive who advised that it would be dangerous for the pilot to fly so close to the ground.

In early March, 1939, Gable received his divorce from Rhea Langham and was free to marry Carole Lombard. The simple Lombard-Gable rites took place in Kingman, Arizona, on March 29, 1939. Gable's appearance as Rhett Butler in *Gone With the Wind,* a role that Lombard had encouraged him to accept, required that the newlyweds return to Los Angeles at the conclusion of the ceremony.

In the summer of 1939, the Gables settled on a twenty-acre estate in the Encino section of the San Fernando Valley about twenty-three miles from Los Angeles. Their white brick two-story colonial residence, formerly the home of Raoul Walsh, was approached by a winding arboreal drive. Together, Lombard and

Clark Gable and Carole Lombard on the day following their marriage in Kingman, Arizona, March 29, 1939.

Lombard shared her husband's interest in hunting and was regarded as a good shot.

Gable shared the responsibilities of "ranch" life. At the ranch Lombard tended to the barnyard animals, while Gable took pleasure in running the tractor, plowing the hillside property.

The Clark Gables treasured quiet evenings at home with perhaps a few close friends, seated in the "gun room" of the Encino ranch. On a visit to the ranch in 1940, historian Henry Pringle observed that the conversation was lively but intelligent, focusing on current politics, the European war, or topics of a lighter and more personal nature. Studio business was not a preferred subject of conversation after sunset. As a rule, Lombard and Gable conducted their business affairs during daylight hours in the office of Jean Garceau, their secretary, on the first floor of the mansion.

The Gables rarely entertained lavishly and were seldom seen at night clubs. Lombard, however, enjoyed professional tennis and often appeared with Gable at the Los Angeles Tennis Club. Lombard learned to share her husband's enjoyment of the outdoors and was his constant companion on hunting trips to the La Grulla Gun Club in the mountains south of Ensenada, Mexico. "She can handle a shotgun as easily as a lipstick," wrote Faith Baldwin in 1939. "She can pile out of bed at five in the morning, yank on boots, wool riding pants, a lumber jacket—not the most becoming of costumes—drink some scalding coffee and start out in a station wagon for a duck blind, over a mile of bumpy road into some God-forsaken wilderness where she'll kneel in mud and water, waiting and motionless, until the wedge-shaped flight of birds passes overhead against the morning sky. And when it's time to eat, it won't be crêpes suzette!" A few hundred feet of home movie film recall one such hunting trip. Images of Lombard appear on the screen, attired in a leather jacket and a pair of old slacks with a rifle balanced precariously on her shoulder, frolicking before a camera held by some forgotten guest more than a quarter of a century ago. Gable regarded Lombard as a good shot, but when she missed her target, everyone in the party could hear her disappointed, "damn!"

Made For Each Other, Lombard's second film for Selznick, was released a month before her marriage to Gable. It was the first of four dramatic roles which Lombard chose before her return to

With Gable and Harry Fleischmann at the La Grulla Gun Club in the mountains south of Ensenada, Mexico.

With Gable at the La Grulla Gun Club, 1940.

comedy in *Mr. and Mrs. Smith* in 1941. Fearful that she would be typed as a comedienne, Lombard wished to demonstrate her considerable skill as a dramatic actress. The failure of *Fools for Scandal* may also have influenced her decision to choose a dramatic story. The only comic relief in *Made For Each Other* was a dinner party scene, superbly directed by John Cromwell, in which the wife, Jane Mason (Lombard), tries to impress the boss, Judge Doolittle (Charles Coburn), that her husband (James Stewart) deserves a promotion. Left to Lombard's Jane, the result is disastrous.

Directed again by Cromwell, Lombard appeared next with Cary Grant in the RKO production, *In Name Only,* based on the novel *Memory of Love* by Bessie Breuer. Kay Francis, in a supporting role, gave an "effectively venomous performance as [Grant's] mercenary wife." Richard Sherman's adaptation, written in a style that might be called romantic realism, presented the story of a young widow who falls in love with a married man. Touches of comedy and melodrama merged to create a pleasing film, popular with audiences and critics. Lombard's struggle with the fishing pole at the beginning of *In Name Only* was delightful. The film editor, William Hamilton, alternated closeup views of the amateur angler, marvelously subtle in expressing her frustration, with glimpses of the fishing line tangled in a tree branch.

Following an appendectomy, Carole Lombard returned to RKO to appear opposite Brian Aherne and Anne Shirley in a hospital drama, *Vigil in the Night,* produced and directed by George Stevens. The film criticized the deficiencies of the English hospital system which was sometimes responsible for the unnecessary loss of life. The film received mixed reviews, although most critics commended Lombard for her portrayal of the sacrificing nurse, Anne Lee.

Continuing at RKO, Lombard appeared opposite Charles Laughton and William Gargan in Robert Ardrey's adaptation of

[33]

the Sidney Howard play, *They Knew What They Wanted*. Lombard gave a sensitive portrayal of the lonely waitress, Amy, who journeys to the Napa Valley to marry a man she has never met. The atmosphere on the set of *They Knew What They Wanted* was not always harmonious. Garson Kanin, a young director with very definite ideas, came into conflict with the strong-willed Charles Laughton. When Kanin, after a disagreement with Laughton, walked off the set one day, the production crew must have wondered if they knew what they wanted. Lombard diplomatically avoided becoming involved in these conflicts, recognizing the preeminence of the director on the film set.

Carole Lombard always enjoyed a happy relationship with the members of the production crew, most of whom she addressed on a first name basis. During the Christmas season Lombard personally selected a gift for each member of the crew employed on her current production. She had a particular fondness for Pat Drew, an electrician who had lost his leg in an airplane accident. Her contracts stipulated that Drew was to be employed as the electrician on all her films. While at work on the set, Lombard sometimes used profanity, a form of expression acquired from her brother Frederick. It was spoken so naturally, however, that it usually brought a chuckle of laughter from the film crew. They appreciated her sharp wit and would not hesitate, when appropriate, to surprise her with a gag gift. The crew respected her, too, as a master of her craft. Harry Stradling, a cinematographer who worked with Lombard, recalled: "She knows as much about the tricks of the trade as I do! In closeup work I wanted to cover her scar simply by focusing the lights on her face so that it would seem to blend with her cheek. She was the one to tell me that a diffusing glass in my lens would do the same job better. And she was right."

Following the completion of *They Knew What They Wanted,* Lombard accompanied Gable to Baltimore where he underwent treatment for a shoulder injury sustained during the filming of *San Francisco* in 1936. Before returning to California, Lombard and Gable stopped in Washington, D.C., and were invited by President Roosevelt to call at the White House. Following a national radio

Director Garson Kanin looks on as Lombard, accompanied by Gable, departs for Napa Valley to appear in the location scenes for They Knew What They Wanted, *1940.*

James Montgomery Flagg's rendering of Carole Lombard.

address, the President talked privately with the Gables, questioning them about film making and the motion picture industry.

Lombard appeared next in a marital comedy, *Mr. and Mrs. Smith,* directed by Alfred Hitchcock from a scenario by Norman Krasna. In his conversations with François Truffaut, Hitchcock recalled that he had agreed to direct the film as a "friendly gesture" to Carole Lombard. Hitchcock, whose genre was melodrama and suspense, never clearly understood Krasna's scenario, mediocre at best, which recounted the experiences of a young Manhattan couple who discover that because of a boundary change they are not legally

married. There were a few funny lines. In the back seat of a taxi, Lombard's Anne, incensed that David has failed to propose, tells him: "I always had a suspicion about you. So did my mother. Your forehead slants back too much." The plush settings, the apartment interiors and Lake Placid resort, were beautifully photographed and underscored with music composed by Edward Ward. The story, unfortunately, never really succeeded.

Having learned that Hitchcock "treated actors like cattle," Lombard surprised the British director by having a small corral constructed in the sound stage. Three young cows, attached with nameplates for Lombard, Montgomery and Gene Raymond, were enclosed in the pen. On another occasion, when Hitchcock announced that he would make a brief appearance in the film, Lombard assumed the task of directing Hitchcock in a scene with Robert Montgomery. Cameramen and technicians laughed when Lombard, seated in the director's chair, ordered Hitchcock to repeat the scene several times. "Give, give," she told the portly director as he crossed in front of Montgomery, tipping his hat. After criticizing his posture and gait, Lombard ordered the sequence printed. Later, she supervised the editing of the episode.

In the winter of 1941, Carole Lombard interrupted a vacation in South Dakota to appear opposite Jack Benny in her last film, *To Be or Not to Be,* produced and directed by Ernst Lubitsch. "I read the script and liked it," she told Thornton Delehanty of the *New York Herald Tribune* in late November, 1941, "and I've always wanted to make a picture with Lubitsch—to say nothing of . . . Jack Benny."

The scenario by Edwin Justus Mayer from a story by Ernst Lubitsch and Melchoir Lengyel was a careful blend of comedy and drama. "I was tired of the two established, recognized recipes," Lubitsch wrote in *The New York Times,* "drama with comedy relief and comedy with dramatic relief. I made up my mind to

make a picture with no attempt to relieve anybody from anything at any time; dramatic when the situation demands it, satire and comedy whenever it is called for. One might call it a tragical farce or a farcical tragedy—I do not care and neither do the audiences."

Under the guidance of Lubitsch, Lombard, as Maria Tura, performed brilliantly. This time, she had an abundance of good dialogue and managed the comic and dramatic situations with incomparable skill. Never was Lombard more radiant and glorious than in *To Be or Not to Be*.

One of the most memorable scenes in *To Be or Not to Be* is the exchange of dialogue between Maria Tura (Lombard) and her husband Joseph, "Poland's greatest actor," played by Jack Benny. Having just completed the Hamlet soliloquy, Joseph rushes into Maria's dressing room, exclaiming: "It happened—what every actor dreads!" Maria, startled, inquires, "What?" Tura answers in a dejected tone, "someone walked out on my monologue. Tell me, Maria, am I losing my grip?" Feeling sorry for him, she tries to be reassuring: "Of course not, darling. I'm so sorry." Tura: "He walked out on me." Maria continues: "Maybe he didn't feel well. Maybe he had a sudden heart attack." Tura: "I hope so." Maria's voice grows stronger: "If he'd stayed, he might have died." Tura, encouraged by Maria's words, replies: "Maybe he's dead already. Oh, darling, you're so comforting." Embracing his wife, Tura concludes, "I wonder if he really got sick? Oh, those terrible doubts!"

Released in February, 1942, *To Be or Not to Be* stimulated critical comment because Lubitsch had used dramatic scenes, especially the bombing of Warsaw, as a background for the portrayal of comic situations. Others were offended by the director's humorous treatment of Nazi brutality. In his reply, Lubitsch justified the humor as proof that the Nazis had become as acquainted with the language of cruelty "as a salesman referring to the sale of a handbag." *To Be or Not to Be*, however, was generally regarded as a brilliant satire that would serve as effective propaganda against the Third Reich.

Following the entry of the United States into World War II in 1941, Clark Gable was named chairman of the Hollywood Victory Committee. In January, 1942, he arranged for Lombard to embark on a bond selling tour that would climax in Indianapolis on January fifteenth. Gable designated Otto Winkler, one of his closest friends and a press agent at MGM, to accompany his wife and Mrs. Elizabeth Knight Peters on the tour. It has been alleged that on the eve of their departure for Indianapolis, Lombard and Winkler had flipped a coin to decide if their return journey would be made by air or train. Winkler, who had wanted to travel by train, is said to have received tails and lost. But Carlton Dufus, in charge of special activities in the Treasury Department's defense stamp drive, reported that Winkler had told him a day or so prior to their return to Los Angeles that Lombard "wanted to go by train so she could make scheduled appearances for us .in Kansas City and Albuquerque, but picture commitments finally forced her to take the plane that cost her life."

Carole Lombard's appearance in Indianapolis on January fifteenth was an outstanding success. Enthusiastic crowds greeted her during the day, and on the steps of the State House in Indianapolis, Lombard sold $2,107,513 worth of government bonds. That evening Lombard traveled by motorcade to Cadle Tabernacle in Indianapolis where she delivered a short, patriotic address. After leading the audience in the singing of *The Star-Spangled Banner,* she raised her arms and spoke publicly for the last time: "Before I say goodbye to you all—come on—join me in a big cheer—V for Victory!" Will Hays, who had accompanied her during the day, recalled that after the rally, "though she was gay and radiant, tears came to her eyes as she once more voiced her gratitude for the reception the people of her native state had given her. The plain fact is, Carole Lombard wanted to serve her country and with all she had, and she did just that."

At four A.M. Friday, January 16, 1942, Lombard, accompanied by her mother and Winkler, arrived at the Indianapolis airport and boarded TWA flight three. The Lockheed Skyclub was scheduled to land in Burbank, California, at 8:30 P.M. When the plane landed in Albuquerque four passengers, including violinist Joseph Szigeti, gave up their seats to make room for fifteen officers and men of the Army Ferrying Command. Flight three continued on to Las Vegas, Nevada, where it landed to refuel at 7:00 P.M. Seven minutes later, in the darkness of a clear night, the silver winged, twin engine aircraft sped down the desert runway to complete the final segment of its transcontinental journey. Veering thirteen degrees off course, pilot Wayne C. Williams ascended to

With Governor H. F. Schricker of Indiana, Will Hays, president of the Motion Picture Producers and Distributors of America, and Eugene C. Pulliam chairman of the Indiana Defense Savings staff in Indianapolis, January 15, 1942.

an altitude of 8,100 feet. Twenty-three minutes later the skyliner crashed into Table Rock Mountain about thirty miles southwest of Las Vegas. Dan Yanish, a watchman at the Blue Diamond Mine near Las Vegas, witnessed the accident from a distance: "I was watching the plane go over our diggings. It was a beautiful, clear night and you could see for miles. It hardly seemed minutes before the plane faded away over the Charleston Range when I saw a flash and then big tongues of flame rising from a mountainside." Upon impact, the tail section telescoped into the nose, cracking in two "like a piece of kindling wood." All twenty-two passengers, including Carole Lombard, died instantly.

Clark Gable arrived in Las Vegas to join the search for his wife. The rugged mountain terrain, overgrown with Joshua and Mesquite, delayed the discovery of the wreckage. Gable journeyed part way with the searchers, but was finally persuaded to return to Las Vegas. On January eighteenth, the body of Carole Lombard was identified "by a wisp of unscorched blond hair" found in the forward section of the fuselage. Two days later Clark Gable, de-

Wreckage of the T.W.A. Sky-Club which crashed into Table Rock Mountain near Las Vegas, Nevada, January 16, 1942, killing Carole Lombard, her mother and twenty other passengers.

The search party returns with the body of Carole Lombard, discovered two days after the crash.

Clark Gable attending the funeral services for his wife and Mrs. Elizabeth Peters in Glendale, California.

scribed as a "man crushed in spirit, a man who has lost all that is dear to him," returned to Los Angeles with the bodies of his wife and Mrs. Peters.

The funeral services for Carole Lombard and her mother were held on January twenty-first in the Church of the Recessional at Forest Lawn Cemetery in Glendale, California. Walter Lang, Harry Fleishman, Fred MacMurray, Buster Collier, Nat Wolff, Al Menasco, Danny Winkler and Zeppo Marx, friends and associates of the actress, served as pallbearers. The Rev. Gordon C. Chapman's eulogy contained a tribute to Carole Lombard and Mrs.

This was Clark Gable's favorite portrait of Carole Lombard. The reverse side carried Lombard's inscription to Gable.

Peters prepared by her closest friends: "Only those are fit to live who do not fear to die, and none are fit to die who have shrunk from the joy and duty of life. Those whom we have come to honor and, in God's name to bless, never shrank from life, but welcomed it—welcomed life and its every aspect—loved life and were responsive to both its duties and its joys. . . . Each believed steadfastly in the glorious life to come."

A host of film notables expressed their grief at the passing of Carole Lombard. Director Tay Garnet noted that Hollywood had "watched her grow from Jane Peters, the high-spirited girl of early studio days, to Carole Lombard, one of Hollywood's most respected actresses. I can only add my respect and grief to that of others who will never forget her." Ginger Rogers believed, too, that the film world had "lost a valuable star who brought joy to millions and her associates have lost a wonderful friend." Joseph Breen of RKO found it difficult to believe that "Carole Lombard will not be seen again in our studios and homes." Claudette Colbert described her as "one of the most genuine personalities in Hollywood." Charles

Carole Lombard's inscription for her husband, Clark Gable, "Pa Dear — — I love you — — Ma," made on the reverse side of a portrait photograph.

Laughton praised her achievements as an actress and expressed his conviction that "Carole Lombard will not be forgotten in Hollywood." Director Edward F. Cline remembered how Carole Lombard "was always there with the sunny smile and helpful hand for her co-workers. Creating happiness was her life work, and she did her job well."

National leaders also paid tribute to Carole Lombard. Secretary of the Treasury Henry Morgenthau described the success of the bond tour and reflected that "she was always glad to respond to any call the Government made upon her, and her spirit of service was an example and an inspiration to many others." Harold N. Graves, assistant to Secretary Morgenthau, stated that Carole Lombard "died while in the service of her country just as surely as did the soldiers who crashed with her." Perhaps the finest tribute to Carole Lombard was contained in a telegram sent by President Franklin D. Roosevelt to Clark Gable: "She is and always will be a star, one we shall never forget, nor cease to be grateful to."

The Films *of*
Carole Lombard

Note

There is no evidence that Carole Lombard appeared in any of the following motion pictures which have, on occasion, been listed in her filmography: *Officer O'Brien* (Pathé, 1929); *Dynamite* (MGM, 1929); *Parachute* (Pathé, 1929); the *Match King* (Warner Bros., 1932).

Lombard did have a role in *The Divine Sinner* (Rayart 1928), sometimes attributed to her, which appears to have been released under another title in late 1928 or 1929. There is no mention of the film under the original title in the *Catalog of Copyright Entries, 1912-1929*. *Divine Sinner,* however, *was* exhibited in New York City at Loew's theatre in September, 1928, as the second feature on a double bill.

It is possible that Lombard had a minor role in *Gold Heels* (Fox, 1925), but this fact could not be documented. It should also be noted that her Sennett filmography is still incomplete. Fourteen Sennett shorts, however, can definitely be attributed to her.

In the biographical section and in the filmography I have adopted a uniform spelling for "Carole," adding the "e". In late adolescence Lombard frequently bruised herself and was advised by a numerologist, a Miss Platt, to add the "e". This occurred shortly after the adoption of her film name in 1925. Studio film magazines and trade publications, however, continued to spell her first name variously until the early 1930s. Following the release of *Fast and Loose* in November, 1930, the studio used the "e" consistently in her screen credits.

A Perfect Crime

Dwan Associates / 1921

CAST

Directed by Allan Dwan. Screenplay by Allan Dwan. From the *Saturday Evening Post* story by Carl Clausen. Photographed by Lyman Broening. Five reels. Released March 5, 1921.
Monte Blue (*Wally Griggs*); Jacqueline Logan (*Mary Oliver*); Stanton Heck ("*Big Bill*" *Thaine*); Hardee Kirkland (*President Halliday*); Jane Peters [Carole Lombard] (*Grigg's sister*).

SYNOPSIS

Bank messenger Wally Griggs is regarded as a nonentity by his fellow workers and the bank president Mr. Halliday. At closing time, however, the drab Mr. Griggs assumes the identity of James Brown, a debonaire young sportsman and teller of adventure tales. Mixing in suburban society Griggs even deceives Mr. Halliday, who is fascinated by Brown's bogus adventure stories.

Griggs falls in love with Mary Oliver who has been cheated out of her inheritance by "Big Bill" Thaine, now District Attorney. Although Griggs loves Mary, he realizes that he could not support her on a salary of $63.00 per week and still provide for his little sister.

When Griggs is given the responsibility of delivering twenty-five thousand dollars in bonds, he hides the certificates in the vault and disappears. Captured a short time later, he sues the city for false arrest. The angry mayor forces Thaine to pay from his personal funds the damages demanded by Griggs, thus restoring Mary's inheritance. Griggs meanwhile recovers the bonds, pretending aphasia. The royalties from Griggs' new adventure book will be an added income, making it possible for Griggs to wed Mary.

REVIEWS

Lawrence Reid,
The Motion Picture News, June 25, 1921:
"Mr. Dwan has made the most of the story and characterization. The flaws, doubtless, appeared in the original script. It offers romance, humor and pathos and keeps moving. Certainly it is a novelty, and there is no doubt that it offers good entertainment."

With Monte Blue.

Marriage in Transit

Fox / 1925

Directed by R. William Neill. From the story by Grace Lutz. Released March 29, 1925.

CAST

Edmund Lowe (*Holden – Cyril Gordon*); Carole Lombard (*Celia Hathaway*); Adolph Milar (*Haynes*); Frank Beal (*Burnham*); Harvey Clarke (*Aide*); Fred Walton (*Valet*); Byron Douglas, Fred Butler, Wade Boteler, Fred Becker, Edward Chandler (*Conspirators*).

SYNOPSIS

Secret agent Cyril Gordon must recover a government code stolen by conspirators. Posing as Holden, the ringleader of the conspirators, whom he closely resembles, Gordon locates the code and escapes. During his flight, Gordon marries Celia Hathaway, Holden's girlfriend, who is ignorant of the agent's real identity. Following the capture of Holden and the conspirators, Celia expresses a sincere affection for Gordon.

REVIEWS

Exhibitor, Chateaugay, New York:
"Used two reel comedy with it. Made a show that pleased everyone who was fortunate to see it."

Exhibitor, Jackson, Wyoming:
"Contrary to my expectations, this one pleased very well."

Exhibitor, Winchester, Indiana:
"The only picture that I have been able to register a box office plus on in quite some time. . . ."

Exhibitor, South Dakota:
"Well directed and entertaining. Carole Lombard good in support."
Lawrence Reid,

Motion Picture News, April 11, 1925:
"For about half its footage this picture gives promise of putting over a clever mystery melodrama. Then it begins to sag and loses its punch while the romantic element is being expressed . . . Edmund Lowe's leading woman, Carole Lombard, displays good poise and considerable charm."

With Edmund Lowe.

[49]

Hearts and Spurs

Fox / 1925

Directed by W. S. Van Dyke. Screenplay by John Stone. From the story by Jackson Gregory. Photographed by Allen Davey. Five reels. Released June 7, 1925.

CAST

Charles [Buck] Jones (*Hal Emory*); Carole Lombard (*Sybil Esta-brook*); William Davidson (*Victor Dufresne*); Freeman Wood (*Oscar Estabrook*); Jean Lamott (*Celeste*); J. Gordon Russell (*Sid Thomas*); Walt Robbins (*Terry Clark*); Charles Eldridge (*The Sheriff*).

With Charles Buck Jones.

SYNOPSIS

Oscar Estabrook incurs a gambling debt to the villainous Victor Dufresne. Dufresne forces Estabrook to pay off his gambling losses by robbing stagecoaches. Having no knowledge of her brother's involvement with Dufresne, Sybil Estabrook, accompanied by her maid, makes a journey west. Soon after her arrival at the ranch, Sybil meets Hal Emory who rescues her from a falling boulder. Emory falls in love with Sybil, saves Estabrook from further wrong-doing, and exposes the dishonest Dufresne who is killed by an avalanche of boulders.

REVIEWS

Laurence Reid,
Motion Picture News, June 20, 1925:
"The melodrama is balanced effectively with comedy relief. . . . The director has shot the story against some picturesque backgrounds and these seem to blend with the action in such a way that it appears convincing in spite of its exaggerations."

With Charles Buck Jones.

Durand of the Badlands

Fox / 1925

Directed by Lynn Reynolds. From the novel by Maibelle Heikes Justice. Five reels. Released November 1, 1925.

CAST

Charles [Buck] Jones (*Dick Durand*); Marion Nixon (*Molly Gore*); Malcolm Waite (*Clem Allison*); Fred De Silva (*Pete Garson*); Luke Cosgrove (*Kingdom Come Knapp*); George Lessley (*John Boyd*); Buck Black (*Jimmie*); Ann Johnson (*Clara Belle Seesel*); James Corrigan (*Joe Gore*); Carole Lombard (*Ellen Boyd*).

SYNOPSIS

Authorities in the West seek to arrest Dick Durand for crimes which he did not commit. Durand becomes friends with Molly Gore whose invalid father is no longer able to work the farm. Pete Garson, a crook, conspires with the villainous Clem Allison, the town's sheriff, to steal a shipment of gold which John Boyd is transfering to the railroad station.

After Garson and the sheriff have stolen the gold, they try to place the blame on Durand. Durand meanwhile, has taken the children of the murdered victims of the holdup to Mary's cottage. Durand escapes and goes to the office of the U.S. Marshall. Establishing his innocence, Durand returns to rescue Boyd's daughter, Ellen, who has been made a prisoner in the mine. Following the arrest of Allison and Garson, Durand, Mary, and the children are happily reunited.

REVIEWS

Chester J. Smith,
Motion Picture News, October 24, 1925:
"Here is a real smart Western with a well-told and well-acted story. Here and there it has a bit of the hackneyed tale characteristic of the Western, but for the most part it fairly sparkles with action and suspense such as is rarely seen in pictures of this type.

"Buck Jones fits into the role·of Durand nicely and his acting brings all the sympathy necessary to the misunderstood and much maligned 'bandit.' But second to the work of the star is that of another Buck—Buck Black, a youngster who plays the part of Jimmy, the orphaned youth who aids Durand through many tough situations. Young Buck acts as naturally as Buck Jones and between them they will hold many an audience spellbound."

The Road to Glory

Fox / 1926

Directed by Howard Hawks. Screenplay by L. G. Rigby from a story by Howard Hawks. Photographed by Joseph August. Running time, 93 minutes. Released February 7, 1926.

CAST

May McAvoy (*Judith Allen*); Leslie Fenton (*David Hale*); Ford Sterling (*James Allen*); Rockliffe Fellowes (*Del Cole*); Milla Davenport (*Aunt Selma*); John Macsweeney (*Butler*).

SYNOPSIS

Judith Allen, the daughter of wealthy James Allen, is engaged to David Hale. Following their marriage, David and Judith have made arrangements to live with the bride's father. During their engagement James Allen is killed in a street accident. A short time later Judith is informed that she will lose her sight because of her involvement in an automobile accident. Embittered, Judith breaks off her engagement with David and retires to the country with a pair of old servants. When the butler informs David that Judith's depression is worsening, he travels through a thunderstorm to be

With Rockcliffe Fellows.

with her. During their conversation, a tree crashes through the roof injuring David. Judith forgets her own troubles and makes every effort to help David. Having saved David's life, her sight is miraculously restored.

REVIEWS

Moving Picture World, February 20, 1926
"Story of a speed-mad girl and the bitter road she followed before finding her real self and happiness."

The Bioscope (London), April 1, 1926:
"Though the story is a little bit morbid, the interest is well maintained and the production and acting are such as to ensure the tears of the sympathetic. It is a film which can hardly fail to appeal, particularly, to the female audience."

Variety, April 28, 1926:
"[Would] make perfect entertainment for any of the neighborhood houses specializing in daily change of program. It might even be worthy of showing before church organizations since half a dozen or more morals and lessons are neatly sugar coated."

The Sennett Comedies

Smith's Pony

Sennett–Pathé / 1927

Two reels. Released September 18, 1927.

CAST

Raymond McKee, Ruth Hiatt, Mary Ann Jackson, Carole Lombard, Billy Gilbert.

The Girl From Everywhere

Sennett–Pathé / 1927

Directed by Edward Cline. Screenplay by Harry McCoy and Vernon Smith. Two reels. Released December 11, 1927.

CAST

Daphne Pollard, Dot Farley, Mack Swain, Carole Lombard, Irwin Bacon, Madalynne Field.

Lombard (center) and other Sennett girls with Buffalo Bill, Jr. (wearing cowboy hat), and Sol Sachs, a Sennett exhibitor from Dallas, Texas.

With Madalynne Field (center) and Daphne Pollard in Run, Girl, Run *(1928).*

Run, Girl, Run

Sennett–Pathé / 1928

Directed by Alf Goulding. From the story by Harry McCoy and James Tynon. Film editor, William Hornbeck. Technicolor sequences. Two reels. Released January 15, 1928.

CAST

Daphne Pollard and Carole Lombard.

SYNOPSIS

At Sunnydale School where pupils learn the three R's, Romeos, Roadsters, and Roller skates, Norma (Carole Lombard) is the star athlete. Although she has broken training, Norma wins a crucial footrace against a rival school. The victory permits the coach (Daphne Pollard) to retain her position at Sunnydale.

The Beach Club

Sennett–Pathé / 1928

Directed by Harry Edwards. From the story by Jefferson Moffitt and Harry McCoy. Two reels. Released January 22, 1928.

CAST

Billy Bevan, Madeline Hurlock, Carole Lombard, Vernon Dent.

The Best Man

Sennett–Pathé / 1928

Directed by Harry Edwards. Supervised by John A. Waldron. Two reels. Released February 19, 1928.

CAST

Billy Bevan, Alma Bennett, Vernon Dent, Carole Lombard, Andy Clyde, Bill Searley.

The Swim Princess

Sennett–Pathé / 1928

Directed by Alf Goulding. Supervised by John Waldron. Screenplay by James T. Tynan and Frank Capra. Film editor, William Hornbeck. Technicolor sequences. Two reels. Released February 26, 1928.

CAST

Daphne Pollard, Andy Clyde, Carole Lombard, Cissie Fitzgerald.

SYNOPSIS

The swim star (Carole Lombard) at a girl's school is put in jail for speeding while on route to a meet with a rival school. With the assistance of Daphne Pollard she escapes from jail and together they proceed to the match, arriving in time to participate in the last relay. The swim star is detained by the pursuing sheriff, but Pollard plunges into the pool and wins the relay for the school.

Advertisement for The Swim Princess *(1928).*

The Bicycle Flirt

With Vernon Dent and Billy Bevan in The Bicycle Flirt *(1928).*

Sennett–Pathé / 1928

Directed by Harry Edwards. From the story by Vernon Smith and Harry McCoy. Two reels. Released March 18, 1928.

CAST

Billy Bevan, Vernon Dent, Dot Farley, Carole Lombard.

SYNOPSIS

An attractive girl is advised by her brother-in-law to disregard her regular boyfriend and find a successful businessman like himself. She decides upon a suitor (Billy Bevan) who courts on a bicycle while hanging on to an automobile. After suffering an accident, he is nursed by the girl in the home of her brother-in-law. When the original boyfriend returns, the suitor is expelled. The story ends happily for everyone but the bicycle flirt.

The Girl From Nowhere

Sennett–Pathé / 1928

Directed by Harry Edwards. From the story by Ewart Adamson and Jefferson Moffitt. Two reels. Released August 5, 1928.

CAST

Daphne Pollard, Dot Farley, Mack Swain, Sterling Holloway, Madalynne Field, Carole Lombard.

SYNOPSIS

A series of comic situations and disturbances involving a wardrobe mistress (Daphne Pollard), a group of movie players, and a temperamental director.

His Unlucky Night

Sennett–Pathé / 1928

Directed by Harry Edwards. Supervised by John A. Waldron. From the story by Vernon Smith and Nick Barrows. Film editor, William Hornbeck. Two reels. Released August 12, 1928.

CAST

Billy Bevan, Vernon Dent, Carole Lombard.

The Campus Vamp

Sennett–Pathé / 1928

Directed by Alf Goulding. From the story by Jefferson Moffitt and Earle Rodney. Two reels. Released September 23, 1928.

CAST

Daphne Pollard, Jefferson Moffitt, Earle Rodney, Carole Lombard.

SYNOPSIS

When the headmistress at a school for girls cancels a student production of *Carmen,* the girls decide to hire a hall and produce their own show. The result is disastrous. The Toreador (Daphne Pollard) survives the chaos long enough to "kill" the front and rear portions of the costumed bull.

The Campus Carmen

Sennett–Pathé / 1928

Directed by Harry Edwards. Two reels. Released November 25, 1928.

With Madalynne Field, Matty Kemp, and Sally Eilers in The Campus Vamp *(1928).*

CAST

Carole Lombard, Sally Eilers, Vernon Dent, Carmelita Geraghty, Matty Kemp, Madalynne Field.

Matchmaking Mamas

Sennett-Pathé / 1929

Directed by Harry Edwards. Supervised by John A. Waldron. From the story by Jefferson Moffitt and Carl Harbaugh. Film editor, William Hornbeck. Two reels. Released March 31, 1929.

CAST

Johnny Burke, Matty Kemp, Sally Eilers, Carole Lombard.

SYNOPSIS

Humorous complications result when a father and mother interfere with the matrimonial plans of their children (Sally Eilers and Carole Lombard).

Lombard (second from left) and the Sennett girls pose with Paul Fielding, a Sennett salesman.

Lombard (wearing neck scarf) with (seated): Vernon Dent, Madeline Hurlock, and Billy Bevan.

The Divine Sinner

A Trem Carr production / 1928

Distributed by Rayart. Directed by Scott Pembroke. Screenplay by Robert Anthony Dillon. From the story by Robert Anthony Dillon. Photographed by Hap Depew. Film editor, J. E. Harrington. Running time, 60 minutes. Released July 15, 1928.

CAST

Vera Reynolds (*Lillia Ludwig*); Nigel De Brulier (*Minister of Police*); Bernard Seigel (*Johann Ludwig*); Ernest Hilliard (*Prince Josef Miguel*); John Peters (*Lugue Bernstorff*); Carole Lombard (*Millie Claudert*); Harry Northrup (*Ambassador D'Ray*); James Ford (*Heinrich*); Alphonse Martel (*Paul Coudert*).

SYNOPSIS

At the close of the First World War, Lillia Ludwig, an Austrian girl, journeys to Paris in search of work. She must have a job in order to support her impoverished parents and blind brother. Finding employment as a designer, Lillia's association with a forger leads to her arrest. Lillia's captors have plotted to discredit Prince Josef Miguel, heir to the throne of an unnamed kingdom. The police agree to release her on condition that she involve the Prince in a scandal. Lillia joins the conspiracy, but after several weeks falls in love with the royal figure. Upon the death of his father, Josef Miguel renounces the throne in order to marry Lillia.

Power

Pathé / 1928

Directed by Howard Higgins. Story and screenplay by Tay Garnett. Titles by John Kraft. Photographed by Peverell Marley. Film editor, Doane Harrison. Assistant director, Robert Fellows. Running time, 60 minutes. Released September 23, 1928.

CAST

William Boyd (*Quirt*); Alan Hale (*Flagg*); Jacqueline Logan (*Lorraine La Rue*); Jerry Drew (*The Menace*); Joan Bennett (*A Dame*); Carole Lombard (*Another Dame*) Pauline Curley (*Still Another Dame*).

SYNOPSIS

Flagg and Quirt are ironworkers on a dam project in the West. Although good friends, they frequently get into arguments about women "since [Flagg's] entry into some woman's front door is usually accompanied by [Quirt's] exit through the back."

When Flagg saves Quirt's life one day, their friendship is cemented anew. The two men, however, became romantically involved with the same woman, Lorraine La Rue. When Lorraine learns that their combined bank accounts total forty-five hundred dollars she tells Flagg and Quirt that her mother requires financial assistance for an "operation." Having promised marriage to both men, Flagg and Quirt fight with revolvers when they arrive at the wedding. Having chased Lorraine to the railway terminal, the two men angrily look on as the train carries her away. Bitterness turns to mirth, however, when they catch sight of a pretty blond on the street.

REVIEWS

Mordaunt Hall,
The New York Times, November 27, 1928:
"This picture is dedicated to the subversive belief that all beautiful young ladies desire is a large bankroll. As an exploitation of the above theory, *Power* manages through most of its length to be quite amusing, if not particularly instructive. It is light and doesn't try to solve any world problems; no more need be said."

Variety, November 28, 1928:
"The title tacked on this Pathé feature must have been selected in an elimination contest run by another company for a third company's production. That's the only plausible explanation for its presence."

With William Boyd.

Me, Gangster

Fox / 1928

Directed by Raoul Walsh. Screenplay by Charles Francis Coe and Raoul Walsh. From the *Saturday Evening Post* story by Charles Francis Coe. Photographed by Arthur Edeson. Running time, 70 minutes. Released October 20, 1928.

CAST

June Collyer (*Mary Regan*); Don Terry (*Jimmy Williams*); Anders Randolf (*Russ Williams*); Stella Adams (*Lizzie Williams*); Al Hill (*Danny*); Burr McIntosh (*Bill Lane, Boss*); Walter James (*Police Captain Dodds*); Gustav von Seyffertitz (*Factory owner*); Herbert Ashton (*Sucker*); Harry Cattle (*Philly Kidd*); Joe Brown (*Joe Brown*); Arthur Stone (*Dan the dude*); Nigel De Brulier (*Danish Looie*); Carole Lombard (*Blonde Rosie*); Bob Perry (*Tuxedo George*).

SYNOPSIS

The criminal life of Jimmy Williams is presented in the form of a diary written by the chief character. Handwritten entries from Williams' diary appear as subtitles on the screen. The diary reveals that Williams once lived in the tenement district near New York's East River. Young Williams, in consort with his pal, Danny, embark on a life of crime when they rob a man and escape from the police. As adults, Williams and Danny become more deeply involved in criminal activity.

When Williams robs a factory owner of a fifty thousand-dollar payroll, he is arrested and sent to prison for two years. At first Williams has no intention of returning the stolen money. The news of his mother's death and the pleading of Mary Regan, his sweetheart, persuade Williams to return the loot.

On the day Williams is paroled, members of the gang follow him to Mary's home. When a fight breaks out the police intervene and arrest the culprits. Williams returns the money and is reunited with Mary.

REVIEW

Mordaunt Hall,
The New York Times, October 22, 1928:
"Through its excellent direction and its careful attention to the realistic atmosphere of New York's east side and prison life, it is an absorbing chronicle that points a moral in a subdued and sane fashion."

Show Folks

Pathé / 1928

Directed by Paul L. Stein. Screenplay by Jack Jungmeyer and George Dromgold. Based on the story by Phillip Dunning. Titles by John Kraft. Photographed by Peverell Marley and Dave Abel. R.C.A. synchronization and sound effects with talking sequences and incidental songs. Assistant director, Robert Fellows. Art direction, Mitchell Leisen. Running time, 70 minutes. Released October 21, 1928.

CAST

Eddie Quillan (*Eddie*); Lina Basquette (*Rita*); Carole Lombard (*Cleo*); Robert Armstrong (*Owens*); Crawford Kent (*McNary*); Bessie Barriscale (*Kitty*).

SYNOPSIS

Eddie and Rita achieve success as a dancing team. They are romantically inclined, but after an argument they break up their act.

Bessie Barriscale and Maurice Black.

With Lina Basquette, Maurice Black, Bessie Barriscale, and Eddie Quillan.

[64]

When Rita reads in a trade paper one day that Eddie is planning to marry another woman, she signs a contract with Owens, a Broadway producer.

Eddie acquires a new dancing partner and is booked for an important show. Eddie's performance, however, is a failure and his partner leaves him. Rita, who has achieved stardom in Owens' revue, learns of what has happened. She falsely tells Eddie that she has been fired and proposes that they revive their dancing act.

The audience applauds the performance of Eddie and Rita. Backstage, between encores, Rita tells Owens that she cannot marry him because of her love for Eddie. Owens agrees to cancel her contract. The story closes with Eddie and Rita taking a final bow.

REVIEWS

Variety, December 12, 1928:
"The 10 minutes or therabouts of dialog at the finish doesn't cover *Show Folks'* earlier failings as a picture, but probably will go a long way with the exhibitor and fairly far with the consumer.

"At last a pair of picture dancers can dance, Miss Basquette should, because that's what she used to do. Quellan, in his first feature after a two-reel comedy past, is a surprise, both as a dancer and all-around performer. Lina [Basquette] is best when dancing."

Motion Picture News, December 15, 1928:
"It is a pretentious offering, which does not fulfill the possibilities it holds out."

Picture Play, March 1929:
"Tolerably interesting, because it is lively without being exciting. . . . Carole Lombard, a very pretty blonde, is worth watching."

With Lina Basquette and Bessie Barriscale.

With Eddie Quillan and Bessie Barriscale.

Ned McCobb's Daughter

Pathé / 1928

Directed by William J. Cowen. Screenplay by Marie Beulah Dix. Based on the play by Sidney Howard. Titles by John Kraft. Photographed by David Abel. Film editor, Anne Banchens. Art direction, Edward Jewell. Production manager, John Rohefs. Sound recorder, Josiah Zuro. R.C.A. synchronized musical score with sound effects. Running time, 71 minutes. Released December 2, 1928.

CAST

Irene Rich (*Carrie McCobb*); Theodore Roberts (*Ned McCobb*); Robert Armstrong (*Babe Callahan*); George Baeraud (*George Callahan*); George Hearn (*Butterworth*); Carole Lombard (*Jennie*); Louis Natheaux (*Kelly*).

SYNOPSIS

Babe uses the home of Carrie McCobb Callahan, his sister-in-law, as a headquarters for the storage and distribution of bootleg whiskey. When Babe's brother George kills a revenue agent, the bootleggers hide the body beneath a pile of apples in the cellar. Carrie, George's wife, has no knowledge of the murder, but tries to warn the brothers when federal agents come to search the premises. Suspense mounts when the girl innocently offers the investigators an apple from the bin where the body is stored. The story concludes with the death by drowning of her guilty husband and the arrest of Babe whom she really loves. Carrie is left alone but it is understood that Babe will come back to her when he has served his sentence.

REVIEWS

Variety, February 20, 1929:
"A fine play transcribed to the screen with notable judgment, a product in the very best mode and a candidate for box office honors."

The Film Spectator (Hollywood), November 10, 1928:
"Cowen does not make his story obvious. As it neared its conclusion my curiosity as to how it was going to end was strong. It had reached that point that all good stories must reach—I could not see how it was going to turn out. . . . Carole Lombard repeats the good impression she made on me in *Show Folks*."

With Irene Rich.

With Billy Bevan, Owen Moore,
William Boyd, Phillips Smalley,
and Diane Ellis.

High Voltage

Pathé / 1929

Directed by Howard Higgins. Story and screenplay by Elliott Clawson. Dialogue by James Gleason. Photographed by John Mescall. Film editor, Doane Harrison. Released June 29, 1920.

CAST

William Boyd, Owen Moore, Carole Lombard, Diane Ellis, Billy Bevan and Phillips Smalley.

With William Boyd, Phillips Smalley, Owen Moore, and Diane Ellis.

With Diane Ellis and William Boyd.

SYNOPSIS

During a snowstorm in the High Sierras, the passengers on a bus, a deputy sheriff and his blonde prisoner, a banker, a bride-to-be, and the driver, find shelter in a cabin occupied by a stranger. When their food supply is exhausted, the group prepares for the worst. Before the party is rescued by an airplane, the stranger, who is also wanted by the police, declares his love for the blonde prisoner.

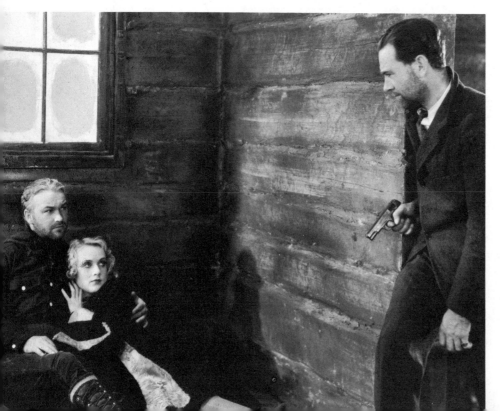

With William Boyd and Owen Moore.

Big News

Pathé / 1929

Directed by Gregory La Cava. Screenplay by Walter De Leon. Dialogue by Frank Reicher. Based on the play, *For Two Cents* by George S. Brooks. Adapted by Jack Jungmeyer. Photographed by Arthur Miller. Talking recorded on film and disc. Film editor, Doane Harrison. Running time, 75 minutes. Released September 7, 1929.

CAST

Robert Armstrong (*Steve Banks*); Carole Lombard (*Mrs. Banks*); Sam Hardy (*Reno*); Tom Kennedy (*Patrolman Ryan*); Louis Payne (*Hansel*); Wade Boetler (*O'Neil*); Charles Sellon (*Editor*).

SYNOPSIS

Steve Banks, addicted to alcohol and the wisecrack, is a dedicated reporter for the *Courier*. When Banks investigates a narcotics ring, Reno, the leader of the gang and an important advertiser in the *Courier,* pressures the publisher to fire him. Having secured a confassion from a Mrs. Perotti implicating Reno in a murder, the

With Robert Armstrong, Warner Richmond, Sam Hardy, and Tom Kennedy.

reporter is restored to his position on the *Courier*. Later, Reno goes to the *Courier* office and listens from across the hall to a conversation between Banks and the editor. After Banks' departure, Reno stabs the editor with a knife left by the reporter. Banks' innocence is established, however, when it is learned that a dictaphone recorded Reno's incriminating conversation with the murder victim.

REVIEWS

Motion Picture News, July 6, 1929:
"Certain tense emotional scenes of *Big News* demanded a feminine player whose beauty and talent must be augmented by a voice capable of giving a sobbing undertone to rapidly spoken lines. Much of the success of the sequence depended upon the sincerity with which this was done.

   "Screen tests were made of several actresses, and Carol (sic) passed the tear-tinged test with flying colors, and was assigned to the role, a powerfully dramatic one which she had greatly coveted."

Film Daily, July 28, 1929:
". . . ranks among [the] best newspaper stories filmed since sound arrived."

Mordaunt Hall,
The New York Times, October 7, 1929:
"Carole Lombard, as the female reporter, is a step above the ingénue film heroine and manages her part with sufficient restraint."

Variety, October 9, 1929:
"As Mrs. Banks . . . Carol (sic) Lombard steps before the camera just often enough to provide the necessary touch and not spoil a good job."

With Robert Armstrong.

With Hedda Hopper.

The Racketeer

Pathé / 1930

Directed by Howard Higgins. Associate producer, Ralph Block. Story and screenplay by Paul Gangelin. Dialogue by A. A. Kline. Photographed by David Abel. Musical director, Josiah Zuro. Sound recorders, A. A. Cutler and Harold Stine. Running time, 66 minutes. Released November 9, 1929.

CAST

Robert Armstrong (*Mahlon Keane*); Carole Lombard (*Rhoda*); Roland Drew (*Tony*); Jeanette Loff (*Millie*); John Loder (*Jack*); Paul Hurst (*Mehaffey*); Winter Hall (*Mr. Simpson*); Winifred

With Roland Drew and Paul Hurst

With Robert Armstrong.

[71]

With Robert Armstrong.

With Roland Drew.

With Robert Armstrong.

Harris (*Mrs. Simpson*); Kit Guard (*Gus*); Al Hill (*Squid*); Bobbie Dunn (*The Rat*); Hedda Hopper (*Mrs. Lee*); Bub Fine (*Weber*).

SYNOPSIS

Rhoda and her sweetheart, Tony, a violinist, receive financial support from Mahlon Keane, a suave racketeer who is attracted to the young blonde. Because of his generosity in arranging a concert for Tony, Rhoda agrees to marry the racketeer.

On the night of the concert, after which Rhoda and Mahlon are to be married, a member of the racketeer's organization kills the leader of a rival gang. Mahlon is killed in a gun battle when the police come to the concert hall to arrest him. Mahlon's death leaves Rhoda free to marry Tony.

REVIEWS

Mordaunt Hall,
The New York Times, January 6, 1930:
"Carol [sic] Lombard speaks her way through the picture as the woman in a sort of dejected key. She is, nevertheless attractive. The picture has a tenseness that held yesterday's audience and drew its applause at the end."

Variety, January 8, 1930:
"Hackneyed, stereotyped production built around the activities and love affairs of a suave bootleg king who drills people for less than a grudge."

Film Daily, January 12, 1930:
"Carole Lombard proves a real surprise, and does her best work to date. In fact this is the first opportunity she has had to prove that she has the stuff to go over. With looks, and a good trouping sense, she also has the personality."

The Arizona Kid

Fox / 1930

Directed by Alfred Santell. Screenplay by Ralph Block and Joseph Wright. From the story by Ralph Block. Photographed by Glen MacWilliams. Incidental music only (not credited). Film editor, Paul Weatherwax. Sound recorder, George Leverett. Running time, 83 minutes. Released May 23, 1930.

CAST

Warner Baxter (*The Arizona Kid*); Mona Maris (*Lorita*); Carole Lombard (*Virginia Hoyt*); Mrs. Jiminez (*Pulga*); Theodore von Eltz (*Nick Hoyt*); Arthur Stone (*Snakebite Pete*); Walter P. Lews (*Sheriff Andrews*); Jack Herrick (*The Hoboken Hooker*); Wilfred Lucas (*His manager*); Hank Mann (*Bartender Bill*); De Sacia Mooers (*Molly*); Larry McGrath (*Homer Snook*); Jim Gibson (*Stage Driver*).

SYNOPSIS

The Arizona Kid, disguised as a traveler, kills a bandit during a stagecoach robbery near Rockville, Arizona. When the stage reaches town, Sheriff Andrews becomes suspicious that the expert marksman may be the notorious Arizona Kid, wanted for various crimes. Anxious to collect the five thousand-dollar reward offered for the

Kid's capture, Andrews make a written request that photographs of the Arizona Kid be forwarded to Rockville.

Although the Kid is in love with Lorita, a dance hall girl, he soon develops an affection for pretty Virginia Hoyt who has come to town with her husband Nick. The Hoyts are a treacherous pair who keep their marriage secret, introducing themselves as brother and sister. When Nick attempts to raid the Kid's secret gold mine, he is shot by the Arizona Kid. Lorita, meanwhile, has robbed the mail pouch, destroying the pictures of the Kid requested by Andrews. Together, Lorita and the Kid make their escape down the arroyo.

REVIEWS

The New York Times, May 17, 1930:
"Carol [sic] Lombard is a beautiful girl, but it is doubtful whether she is suited to the role of Virginia."

Photoplay, July, 1930:
"This is Warner Baxter's follow on his first smash talkie, *In Old Arizona,* and he's just as fine and fascinating as ever. Mona Maris, opposite, is a delightful Spanish sweetheart. a great treat for Baxter fans . . . Wilfred Lucas and Carole Lombard do well with disagreeable roles."

With Warner Baxter.

With Josephine Dunn, Virginia Bruce, Charles "Buddy" Rogers, and Kathryn Crawford.

Safety in Numbers

Paramount / 1930

Directed by Victor Schertzinger. Screenplay by Marion Dix. From the story by George Marion, Jr., and Percy Heath. Photographed by Henry Gerrard. Songs and lyrics by Marion and Richard A. Whiting. Songs: "My Favorite Just Passed"; "The Pickup"; Business Girl"; "Pepola"; "I'd Like to Be a Bee in Your Boudoir"; "You Appeal to Me"; "Do You Play, Madame?" Dances and ensembles directed by David Bennett. Film editor, Robert Bassler. Running time, 60 minutes. Released June 7, 1930.

CAST

Charles "Buddy" Rogers (*William Butler Reynolds*); Kathryn Crawford (*Jacqueline*); Joseph Dunn (*Maxine*); Carole Lombard (*Pauline*); Geneva Mitchell (*Cleo Careine*); Roscoe Karns (*Bertram Shipiro*); Francis McDonald (*Phil Kempton*); Virginia Bruce (*Alma McGregor*); Richard Tucker (*F. Carstair Reynolds*); Raoul Paoli (*Jules*); Lawrence Grant (*Commodore Brinker*); Louise Beavers (*Messaline*).

SYNOPSIS

Twenty-year-old William Butler Reynolds of San Francisco will inherit three hundred and fifty million dollars on his next birthday.

Reynold's uncle is convinced that his nephew, who aspires to be a songwriter, should receive more education in the "ways of the world." To help young Reynolds with his "education," the uncle employs three follies girls, Jacqueline Maxine and Pauline, to guide him around New York.

Arriving in New York, Reynolds writes a new song for a revue

With Josephine Dunn, Charles "Buddy" Rogers, Kathryn Craw-ford, and Virginia Bruce.

With Josephine Dunn, Charles "Buddy" Rogers, Kathryn Crawford, and Francis MacDonald.

in which the girls are to appear. When he demands that the girls receive a raise in salary, the producer fires them and discards Reynolds' music. Later, the producer reconsiders; he restores the song and agrees to give the girls a wage increase. Jacqueline, Maxine and Pauline fulfill their mission as bodyguards when they rescue Reynolds from an unscrupulous chorus girl. All three have grown to find him attractive, but in the end Jacqueline and the millionaire declare their love for one another.

REVIEWS

Mordaunt Hall,
The New York Times, May 31, 1930:
"*Safety in Numbers* is so ridiculous that consideration of its merits can only be given to some charming musical interludes that are skillfully woven into the film."

Variety, June 4, 1930:
"The Schertzinger direction is satisfactory in every department. Interpolation of a silhouette dance flash, strictly revue idea, into a play with music again evidences the elastic advantages of the screen in presenting dialog scenarios with theme songs over the paralleling stage limitations of the average play-with-music (this latter as distinguished from the musical comedy)."

Robert Hage,
The Motion Picture Herald, June 7, 1930:
"Here's that rare combination of intelligent direction, brilliant dialogue—and rich humor. The result is a picture that is entertainment plus."

Lombard, second from the left, on the cover of a song sheet advertising Safety in Numbers.

[77]

With Frank Morgan and Charles Starrett.

Fast and Loose

Paramount / 1930

Directed by Fred Newmeyer. Screenplay by Doris Anderson. Dialogue by Preston Sturges. Based on the play, *The Best People*, by David Gray. Photographed by William Steiner. Dialogue director, Bertram Harrison. Recording engineer, C. A. Tuthill. Running time, 70 minutes. Released November 8, 1930.

CAST

Miriam Hopkins (*Marion Lenox*); Carole Lombard (*Alice O'Neil*); Frank Morgan (*Bronson Lenox*); Charles Starrett (*Henry Morgan*); Henry Wadsworth (*Bertie Lenox*); Winifred Harris (*Carrie Lenox*); Herbert Yost (*George Grafton*); David Hutcheson (*Lord Rockingham*); Ilka Chase (*Millie Montgomery*).

SYNOPSIS

Wealthy Bronson Lenox is informed that his son Bertie has become involved with a show girl, Alice O'Neil. After a visit to the night club where Alice performs in a chorus, the conventional but demo-

With Frank Morgan and Henry Wadsworth.

cratic Lenox is satisfied that she is a fine girl. The snobbish Mrs. Lenox, however, is furious when she learns of her son's love for the entertainer. Matters are further complicated when the parents are informed that their daughter Marion is in love with an automobile mechanic, Henry Morgan.

The elders undergo a change of attitude, however, when the chorus girl and the mechanic decline to marry the Lenox children. Mrs. Lenox works to encourage the wedding, insulted that Alice and Henry should not be eager to wed the children of such an elite family. Everyone is happy when the young people "stage a strictly modern double wedding."

REVIEWS

Mordaunt Hall,
The New York Times, December 1, 1930:
"Praise of photography invariably means that it is the only virtue of the film under consideration. *Fast and Loose,* the pictorial version of the play *The Best People,* which is now adorning the Paramount screen, is an exception, however, for it is not only an example of brilliant camera work, but also a highly amusing feature, with competent acting."

With Henry Wadsworth.

Motion Picture, March 1931:
"A rich girl falls in love with a poor boy, and a rich boy falls in love with a poor girl—with complications. An uneven comedy, bringing to the screen Miriam Hopkins of Broadway."

[79]

It Pays to Advertise

Paramount / 1931

Directed by Frank Tuttle. Screenplay by Arthur Kober. Based on the play by Roi Cooper Megrue and Walter Hackett. Photographed by Archie J. Stout. Running time, 66 minutes. Released February 28, 1931.

CAST

Norman Foster (*Rodney Martin*); Carole Lombard (*Mary Grayson*); Skeets Gallagher (*Ambrose Peale*); Eugene Pallette (*Cyrus Martin*); Lucien Littlefield (*Adams*); Helen Johnson (*Comtesse de Beaurien*); Louise Brooks (*Thelma Temple*); Morgan Wallace (*Donald McChesney*); Marcia Manners (*Miss Murke*); Tom Kennedy (*Perkins*); Junior Coghlan (*Office boy*); John Howell (*Johnson*); John Sinclair (*Window cleaner*).

SYNOPSIS

Assisted by Mary Grayson, a secretary, and Ambrose Peale, an advertising expert, Rodney Martin becomes his father's rival in the

With Eugene Pallette, Norman Foster, and Skeets Gallagher.

With Norman Foster.

soap business. In their advertising campaign Martin and Peale publicize a soap product labeled, "Thirteen—unlucky for dirt." Although the publicity campaign is a huge success, young Martin is financially unable to produce any soap. To prevent his competitor, Adams, from purchasing the popular trade mark, Cyrus Martin pays his son a handsome price for "Thirteen." Mary and Rodney have meanwhile fallen in love.

REVIEWS

Mordaunt Hall,
The New York Times, February 21, 1931:
"*It Pays to Advertise,* the current feature at the Paramount, kept an audience yesterday in a thoroughly good-natured mood. Its humor is seldom overwhelmingly novel, but it succeeded in arousing laughter—which is, after all, the main idea in such productions. There are moments when this farce-comedy gets into deep water by going beyond reasonable bounds, but the characters involved go blissfully on, knowing full well that the plans of the director and others are going to result in general celebration after the final fadeout."

Theatre Magazine, April, 1931:
"Although slightly outmoded and rather obvious for this sophisticated generation, *It Pays to Advertise* is still good fun. It is an hilarious fairytale with a wicked ogre of a father, a Prince Charming of a son, a commercial Merlin, who works magic with advertising, and a lovely girl who suffers for her Prince until the end of the story brings happiness for them. . . . The old stage play has been jazzed up considerably and the picture is capably acted. Miss Lombard is an excellent and appealing secretary."

Photoplay, August 1931:
"The old stage play revamped for the talkies with plenty of speed and lots of laughs. Skeets Gallagher, Norman Foster and Carole Lombard head a perfect cast."

With William Powell.

Man of the World

Paramount / 1931

Directed by Richard Wallace and Edward Goodman. Story and screenplay by Herman J. Mankiewicz. Photographed by Victor Milner. Recording engineer, H. M. Lindgren. Runnting time, 74 minutes. Released March 28, 1931.

CAST

William Powell (*Michael Wagstag*); Carole Lombard (*Mary Kendall*); Wynne Gibson (*Irene*); Guy Kibee (*Harold Taylor*); Lawrence Gray (*Frank Thompson*); Tom Ricketts (*Mr. Bradkin*); Andre Cheron (*Victor*); George Chandler (*Fred*); Tom Costello (*Spade*); Maud Truax (*Mrs. Jowitt*).

SYNOPSIS

Michael Wagstag blackmails wealthy Americans stopping in Paris. Irene, his attractive accomplice, finds a suitable victim in Mary Kendall, an American debutante. Wagstag proceeds to carry out his blackmail scheme but after several weeks the extortionist and the debutante fall in love.

With William Powell.

With William Powell and Guy Kibbee.

Wagstag confesses his past to Mary, but when he attempts to break with Irene, she threatens to call the police. Irene tries to convince him that he will never be free of the past. Persuaded that a life with Mary is impossible, Wagstag is encouraged by Irene to demand $10,000 from Harold Taylor, Mary's uncle. Taylor pays the money while Mary, thinking Wagstag dishonest, sails home with her fiance, Frank Thompson. Wagstag and Irene take passage on a tramp steamer bound for South Africa. On board ship, Wagstag tears up Taylor's check.

REVIEWS

Mordaunt Hall,
The New York Times, March 21, 1931:
"Man of the World . . . is a competently acted piece of work, particularly by Mr. Powell, the beatiful Carole Lombard and Guy Kibbee."

Variety, March 25, 1931:
"Here is an odd story for the screen, written by Herman Mankiewicz and probably expressly for the screen's Powell. . . . Both women, Carole Lombard and Wynne Gibson, the latter especially, added helpful support, along with Guy Kibbee . . . in his first talker."

Photoplay, July, 1931:
"A good picture; not much action but plenty of drama and a great performance by William Powell. Carole Lombard is the lonely heroine."

Ladies' Man

Lombard adjusts her makeup before beginning a scene in Ladies' Man.

Paramount / 1931

Directed by Lothar Mendes. Screenplay by Herman J. Mankiewicz. Dialogue by Herman J. Mankiewicz. Based on the story by Rupert Hughes. Photographed by Victor Milner. Recording engineer, H. M. Lindgreen. Running time, 70 minutes. Released May 9, 1931.

CAST

William Powell (*James Darricott*); Kay Francis (*Norma Page*); Carole Lombard (*Rachel Fendley*); Gilbert Emery (*Horace Fendley*); Olive Tell (*Mrs. Fendley*); Martin Burton (*Anthony Fendley*); John Holland (*Peyton Weldon*); Frank Atkinson (*Valet*); Manda Turner Gordon (*Therese Bianton*).

SYNOPSIS

Wealthy women with boring husbands are attracted to the debonair James Darricott. Darricott derives a substantial income from the sale of jewelry he receives from his women admirers.

Darricott becomes involved with the middle-aged Mrs. Fendley from whom he receives expensive gifts, which are converted into cash. Although Rachel Fendley knows of her mother's association with Darricott, she too falls in love with him. Darricott, however, is attracted to only one woman, Norma Page.

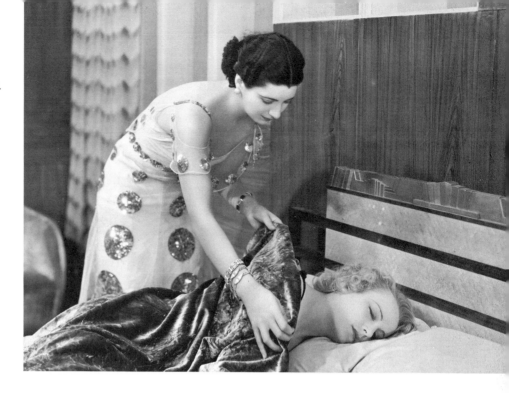

With Kay Francis.

Learning of his wife's infidelity, the jealous Mr. Fendley has a fight with Darricott in the latter's apartment. Darricott falls to his death from the window while Norma, the only woman he really loved, speaks his epitaph on the sidewalk below. A short time later, Mr. Fendley gives himself up to the police.

REVIEWS

Motion Picture, April, 1931:
"After the subtle comedy handling of the picture the tragic ending is unexpected and a trifle disconcerting. Lothar Mendes has dissected this Rupert Hughes story in a rather daring manner, which with its ultramodern setting make it film fare for the sophisticates rather than for grandma."

With Gilbert Emery.

*With Olive Tell and
William Powell.*

André Sennwald,
The New York Times, May 1, 1931:
"Mr. Powell receives capable support from the others in the cast.
Kay Francis appears as the girl he loves, Carole Lombard is Rachel
Fendley, Olive Tell is Mrs. Fendley and Gilbert Emery is the out-
raged banker-husband."

Photoplay, August, 1931:
"William Powell, as a sympathetic and attractive gigolo, charms
Olive Tell, Carole Lombard and Kay Francis. Entertaining picture."

*With William Powell and
Martin Burton.*

With Norman Foster.

Up Pops the Devil

Paramount / 1931

Directed by Edward Sutherland. Screenplay by Arthur Kober and Eve Unsell. Based on the play, *Up Pops the Devil,* by Albert Hackett and Francis Goodrich. Photographed by Karl Struss. Dialogue, Arthur Kober, Eve Unsell. Sound recording, Harold Lewis. Running time, 75 minutes. Released May 30, 1931.

CAST

Richard Gallogher (*Biney Hatfield*); Stuart Erwin (*Stranger*); Carole Lombard (*Anne Merrick*); Lilyan Tashman (*Polly Griscom*); Norma Foster (*Steve Merrick*); Edward J. Nugent (*George Kent*); Theodor von Eltz (*Gilbert Morrell*); Joyce Compton (*Luella May Carroll*); Eulalie Jensen (*Mrs. Kent*); Harry Beresford (*Mr. Platt*); Effie Ellsler (*Mrs. Platt*); Sleep N. Eat (*Laundryman*); Guy Oliver (*Waldo*); Pat Moriarity (*Kelly*); Matty Roubert (*Subscription boy*).

SYNOPSIS

Steve Merrick, an aspiring young writer, and his wife Anne, live in

With "Sleep N. Eat."

With Norman Foster and Joyce Compson.

Greenwich Village. Merrick is encouraged in his writing by Gilbert Morrell, a publisher. Morrell sends Merrick an advance on royalties when the author completes two chapters of the novel he is writing. The publisher, however, insists that Merrick spend more time on his writing. To help her husband, Anne goes to work at the local Paramount as a dancer in a revue. At the apartment, household chores and intruders distract Merrick from his literary endeavors. The author, however, finds one visitor, Luella May Carroll, particularly attractive.

Morrell, meanwhile, shows his affection for Anne by giving her money which she accepts as a further advance on her husband's book. Merrick grows suspicious of his wife's relationship with Morrell, while Anne learns of her husband's flirtation with Luella May. After an argument, the Merricks, who really love one another, separate. Several months later, after having achieved fame as a novelist, Merrick returns to the apartment and is reunited with Anne.

REVIEWS

Mordaunt Hall,

The New York Times, May 16, 1931:
"The shining light of this film is Miss Lombard, whose sincerity in her portrayal is only surpassed by her exquisite beauty."

International Photographer, June, 1931:
"Carole Lombard has an abundance of opportunity here, one of the best that has been given her—and what she does with it is a delight. She is seen in moods gay and grave—as to the latter her role at times taking her into the realm of the deeply emotional. . . . She is a real actress."

Photoplay, August, 1931:
"Young love and its struggles neatly handled by Norman Foster, as a young author, and his wife, played by Carole Lombard. Sprightly dialogue."

With director Edward Sutherland (seated).

With Gary Cooper.

I Take This Woman

Paramount / 1931

Directed by Marion Gering and Slavko Vorkapich. Screenplay by Vincent Lawrence. Based on the novel, *Lost Ecstasy,* by Mary Roberts Rinehart. Photographed by Victor Milner. Recording engineer, Earl S. Hayman. Running time, 74 minutes. Released June 27, 1931.

CAST

Gary Cooper (*Tom McNair*); Carole Lombard (*Kay Dowling*); Helen Ware (*Aunt Bessie*); Lester Vail (*Herbert Forrest*); Charles Trowbridge (*Mr. Dowling*); Clara Blandick (*Sue Barnes*); Gerald Fielding (*Bill Wentworth*); Albert Hart (*Jake Mallory*); Guy Oliver (*Sid*); Syd Saylor (Shorty); Mildred Van Dorn (*Clara Hammell*); Leslie Palmer (*Phillips*); Ara Haswell (*Nora*); Frank Darien (*Station agent*); David Landau (*Circus boss*).

SYNOPSIS

Because of her involvement in an innocent scandal in New York, Kay Dowling is ordered by her father to move to the family ranch out west. Arriving at the ranch, Kay has a disagreeable encounter with Tom McNair, an obstinate but good-natured cowboy who refuses to follow her orders. To defeat McNair, Kay becomes more affectionate. She eventually marries the cowboy, but regards him only as a new thrill.

Kay and Tom attempt ranching on their own. The arduous life of the cattle ranch, however, begins to have a corrosive effect on their marriage. After a year Kay separates from her husband

and returns to the comforts of the urban east. McNair leaves the ranch also, becoming a stunt rider in a rodeo. Although Kay has divorced the cowboy, she still loves him. One night during a rodeo performance attended by Kay, McNair is thrown from a horse and seriously injured. The cowboy, who is told that he will never be able to ride again, is reunited with Kay.

REVIEWS

The New York Times, June 13, 1931:
"Quite an entertaining talking picture called *I Take This Woman* . . . is now on view at the Paramount. Eastern beauty is represented in it by the radiant Carole Lombard and the Lochinvar who comes out of the West is portrayed by the gaunt Gary Cooper. . . . Miss Lombard gives a capable performance."

Variety, June 16, 1931:
"A few more performances like this from Carole Lombard and Paramount will have a new star on its list. But some better talkers than *I Take This Woman* would ease the climb. This is a combination western and drawing room affair. It looks expensive and probably won't lose. . . .

"While Miss Lombard plays a snippy and snobby eastern rich girl, and though her eventual submission to the young cowhand doesn't completely overcome some of the dislikeable things she says and does, she climbs on top of the part and becomes a distinct personality. She has a face that photographs from all angles and in her playing never falters. Miss Lombard ought to advance rapidly from this point."

Photoplay, August, 1931:
"That wheezy old plot about the pampered society darling who falls for and marries the rugged cowhand on pappy's ranch comes alive again. But not very. Gary Cooper, looking none too well, and Carole Lombard, miscast, do their best. But when it's all over, it's just another movie. You'll get a surprise though, seeing lovely Carole's beauty sunk as the ranch drudge-of-all-work."

With Charles Trowbridge, Gary Cooper, and Syd Saylor.

No One Man

Paramount / 1932

Directed by Lloyd Corrigan. Screenplay by Sidney Buchman, Agnes Bran Leahy, and Percy Heath. Based on the novel, *No One Man*, by Rupert Hughes. Photographed by Charles Lang. Running time, 73 minutes. Released January 30, 1932.

CAST

Carole Lombard (*Penelope Newbold*); Ricardo Cortez (*Bill Hanaway*); Paul Lukas (*Dr. Karl Bemis*); Juliette Compton (*Sue Folsom*); George Barbies (*Alfred Newbold*); Virginia Hammond (*Mrs. Newbold*); Arthur Pierson (*Stanley McIlvaine*); Francis Moffett (*Delia*); Irving Bacon (*License clerk*).

SYNOPSIS

Wealthy Penelope Newbold, a divorcée, is not sure of what she is

With Paul Lukas and Ricardo Cortez.

seeking in marriage. Penelope shows affection for a Viennese physician, Dr. Karl Bemis, who tries to help her understand herself. Terribly confused, Penelope finds Bemis attractive, but marries a worthless young man, Bill Hanaway, who becomes involved with Sue Folsom. Realizing her mistake, Penelope and Bemis are reunited following Hanaway's death from a heart attack.

With Ricardo Cortez and
Irving Bacon.

REVIEWS

Variety, January 20, 1932:
"Miss Lombard, as the figure around which everything revolves, has a two-way handicap to overcome for sympathy. One is the character she plays and the other is the camera. The lens has been none too kind to her here. Gorgeous in 'stills,' the reproduction on the screen for her is such as to cause audible unfavorable comment from women in the audience."

Mordaunt Hall,
The New York Times, January 23, 1932:
"As the silken heroine, Carole Lombard is required to exhibit some extraordinary psychological reactions. Ricardo Cortez's portrait of the playboy is amusing and Paul Lukas is good in the thinly written part of the physician."

Motion Picture Herald, January 30, 1932:
"The audience at the New York Paramount gave every evidence of having been well entertained by the adaptation and quite satisfied with the work of Miss Lombard, blonde and attractive."

With Ricardo Cortez, Paul Lukas, and Irving Bacon.

Sinners in the Sun

Paramount / 1932

Directed by, Alexander Hall. Screenplay by Vincent Lawrence, Waldemar Young and Samuel Hoffenstein. Based on the story, "The Beachcomber," by Mildred Crain. Photographed by Ray June. Running time, 70 minutes. Released May 13, 1932.

CAST

Carole Lombard (*Doris Blake*); Chester Morris (*Jimmie Martin*); Adrienne Ames (*Claire Kinkaid*); Alison Skipworth (*Mrs. Blake*); Walter Byron (*Eric Nelson*); Reginald Barlow (*Mr. Blake*); Zita (*Mrs. Florence Nelson*); Cary Grant (*Ridgeway*); Luke Cosgrove (*Grandfather Blake*); Ida Lewis (*Grandmother Blake*); Russ Clark (*Fred Blake*); Frances Moffett (*Mrs. Fred Blake*); Pierre De Romey (*Louis*); Veda Buckland (*Emma*); Rita La Roy (*Lil*).

SYNOPSIS

Doris Blake, ambitious and hardworking, models clothes in an exclusive shop. She is in love with Jimmy Martin, an automobile mechanic. Although fond of Martin, Doris refuses to marry him until he has saved enough money to open his own garage. The postponement of the marriage creates conflict and after a quarrel Doris and Martin break their engagement.

Martin becomes a chauffeur to wealthy Claire Kinkaid, whom he eventually marries. In Claire's society, however, the former mechanic is uncomfortable in speech and manner. It is not long before Martin leaves her to become an automobile salesman.

While attending a fashion show at an Eastern Long Island estate, Doris becomes acquainted with the socially prominent Eric Nelson who is separating from his wife. Doris becomes Nelson's mistress and is provided with a luxurious apartment. Although she receives expensive gifts from Nelson, Doris cannot forget Martin, her true love.

Leaving Nelson, Doris goes to work as a cutter in a garment factory. Later, Martin comes to the factory, and the two young people are happily reunited.

REVIEWS

Mordaunt Hall,
The New York Times, May 14, 1932:
"Feminine fashions, fast automobiles and fine wines come to the fore in the course of the happenings in *Sinners in the Sun,* a pictorial adaptation of Mildred Cram's story, *The Beachcomber,* which is now at the Paramount. . . . Miss Lombard acts competently. Mr. Morris is miscast. In spite of her thankless role, Miss Ames does efficient work. Miss Skipworth makes the most of the part of Doris's sympathetic mother and Walter Byron is capable as Nelson."

Variety, May 17, 1932:
"This thesis has been told on the screen too frequently, and usually better than in *Sinners in the Sun.* A very weak picture with an unimpressive future before it.

"Carole Lombard and Chester Morris are paired in the two main roles. They are called upon to make believable a script which sinks from its own weight."

Motion Picture, August, 1932:
"Carole Lombard, a dress model, and Chester Morris, a mechanic, are in love—but she weds a millionaire, and he weds a millionairess, just for spite. Carole's acting is not on a par with her dresswearing ability. Or is the story to blame?"

With Chester Morris.

With Cary Grant.

With Pat O'Brien.

Virtue

Columbia / 1932

Directed by Edward Buzzell. Screenplay by Robert Riskin. Based on the story by Ethel Hill. Photographed by Joseph Walker. Assistant director, Sam Nelson. Sound recorder, Edward Bernds. Running time, 69 minutes. Released October 25, 1932.

CAST

Carole Lombard (*Mae*); Pat O'Brien (*Jimmy*); Ward Bond (*Frank*); Willard Robertson (*MacKenzie*); Shirley Grey (*Gert*); Ed Le Saint (*Magistrate*); Jack La Rue (*Toots* [*gunman*]); Mayo Methot (*Girl friend of Toots*).

SYNOPSIS

Mae and a group of other street girls receive suspended sentences in a New York court on condition they leave the city. Having journeyed as far as 125th Street, Mae meets Jimmy, a taxi driver, who coveys her back downtown. During the ride, Jimmy peppers his conversation with wisecracks and candid observations about women.

With Pat O'Brien.

Jimmy and Mae become better acquainted and under his influence the street walker reforms. After a brief courtship, Mae and Jimmy are married. The police come for Mae on her wedding night, but Jimmy stands by her.

Later, Mae goes to a hotel she used to frequent to collect a two hundred-dollar loan made to her girlfriend. At first Jimmy assumes that she has returned to her old ways. When a murder is committed in the hotel and Mae is arrested, Jimmy, realizing that she has been honest with him, establishes her innocence.

REVIEWS

Mordaunt Hall,
The New York Times, October 25, 1932:
"To the part of little Mae, Carole Lombard brings her alabaster beauty and her talent for looking cruel and tender at the same time."

Variety, November 1, 1932:
"While audience won't go into raves, picture will sufficiently entertain to rate as an attraction worthier than the general run in its class."

No More Orchids

Columbia / 1932

Directed by Walter Lang. Screenplay by Gertrude Purcell. Based on the story by Grace Perkins. Adaptation by Keene Thompson. Photographed by Joseph August. Assistant director, Sam Nelson. Recording engineer, Edward Bernds. Running time, 74 minutes. Released November 25, 1932.

CAST

Carole Lombard (*Anne Holt*); Walter Connolly (*Bill Holt*); Louise Closser Hale (*Grandma*); Lyle Talbot (*Tony*); Allen Vincent (*Dick*); Ruthelma Stevens (*Rita*); C. Aubrey Smith (*Cedric*); William V. Mong (*Burkhart*); Charles Mailes (*Merriwell*); Jameson Thomas (*Prince Carlos*); Harold Minjir (*Modiste*); Sidney Bracey (*Holmes*); Ed Le Saint (*Captain*).

SYNOPSIS

When Anne Holt informs her father that she is in love with Tony, an attractive but penniless bachelor, Mr. Holt is prepared to make every sacrifice for his daughter's happiness.

Anne's uncle Cedric, however, is resolved that his niece will marry a titled foreigner. When his bank faces financial ruin, Mr. Holt appeals to Cedric for a loan. Cedric, however, refuses to grant the loan unless Anne consents to marry Prince Carlos. She

With Lyle Talbot.

With Lyle Talbot, Walter Connolly, and Louise Closser Hale.

agrees, but before the marriage Holt and Grandma arrange a meeting between Anne and Tony in the country. Having prepared for a long journey, Holt flies off in an airplane. Secure in the knowledge that his life insurance policy will provide funds for the bank, leaving Anne free to marry Tony, Holt crashes the plane.

REVIEWS

Variety (Preview), November 18, 1932:
"A smart, polished production replete with good acting, smooth direction and clever lines, having the curse of a suicide at the finish which takes the edge off the otherwise happy finale and leaves a slightly dark brown taste in the mouth. Careful cutting to quicken the self-destruction act, now too long drawn out, should help shape *No More Orchids* to a more satisfactory ending. . . .

"Something a little forced and overstrained in Carole Lombard's delivery, but her clothes and looks carry her through. . . .

"Script sparkles, with Keene Thompson's adaptation and Gertrude Purcell's dialog deserving of bows."

Mordaunt Hall,
The New York Times, January 2, 1933:
"Walter Connolly gives another excellent characterization in the Roxy screen contribution, *No More Orchids,* an unimportant but frequently entertaining picture. Carole Lombard, whose attractive shadow is adorning the Paramount's film, *No Man of Her Own,* also is the principal feminine player in *No More Orchids.*"

*With Clark Gable and
Dorothy Mackaill*

No Man of Her Own

Paramount / 1932

Directed by Wesley Ruggles. Screenplay by Maurine Watkins and Milton Gropper. Based on the story by Edmund Goulding and Benjamin Glazer. Photographed by Leo Tover. Running time, 76 minutes. Released December 1932.

CAST

Clark Gable (*Jerry "Babe" Stewart*); Carole Lombard (*Connie Randall*); Dorothy Mackaill (*Kay Everly*); Grant Mitchell (*Vane*); George Barbier (*Mr. Randall*); Elizabeth Patterson (*Mrs.*

With Clark Gable.

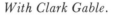
With Clark Gable.

Randall); Farrell MacDonald (*Dickie Collins*); Tommy Conlon (*Willie Randall*); Walter Walker (*Mr. Morton*); Paul Ellis (*Vargas*); Lilian Harmer (*Mattie*); Frank McGlynn, Sr. (*Minister*).

With Clark Gable.

SYNOPSIS

Wealthy gentlemen are enlisted by Kay Everly to play poker with Babe Stewart, a crooked gambler. Although detective Collins has the gambler under close surveillance, he lacks the evidence to make an arrest. Later, when Stewart senses that Collins is closing in on him, he decides to leave town. Stewart selects the little town of Glendale, within commuting distance from New York, as a hiding place.

In Glendale, Stewart meets Connie Randall, the local librarian, who finds the out-of-town gentleman most attractive. On the flip of a coin, Stewart and Connie get married. The gambler regards the marriage as something of a joke, but Connie is quite serious and very much in love.

With Elizabeth Patterson.

With Clark Gable.

Returning to New York, Stewart is again the nightly host at a dishonest poker game. At first Connie believes that her husband is a Wall Street broker, but gradually she learns the truth.

When Kay Everly returns from the Caribbean, she learns of Stewart's marriage to Connie and threatens to go to the District Attorney. Babe, however, has fallen in love with Connie and decides

With Grant Mitchell.

[102]

With Dorothy Mackaill.

to give himself up. Stewart is sentenced to jail for three months. During this absence he tries to make Connie believe that he is in South America on business. After his release Babe and Connie are reunited.

REVIEWS

Mordaunt Hall,
The New York Times, December 31, 1932:
"Miss Lombard and Mr. Gable are amusing and competent players. Between them they keep a rather usual sort of melodrama hustling along at a lively clip and sustain a pleasing illusion of handsome romantics and dashing humor."

Photoplay, March, 1933:
"Clark Gable devotees and fanciers of Carole Lombard should take to this one. Gable in his best heart-fluttering way, and Carole, with lines as scintillant as her person and clothes, turn in delicious love-making episodes that more than redeem the story, a rubber-stamp affair about a card sharper who reforms for love. Fine support, particularly by Grant Mitchell, Elizabeth Patterson and Dorothy Mackaill."

With Clark Gable.

With Jack Oakie, Adrienne Ames, and Sidney Blackmer.

From Hell to Heaven

Paramount / 1933

Directed by Erle C. Kenton. Screenplay by Percy Heath and Sidney Buchman. Based on the drama by Lawrence Hazard. Photographed by Henry Sharp. Running time, 70 minutes. Released February 24, 1933.

CAST

Carole Lombard (*Colly Tanner*); Jack Oakie (*Charlie Bayne*); Adrienne Ames (*Joan Burt*); David Manners (*Wesley Burt*); Sidney Blackmer (*Cuff Billings*); Verna Hillie (*Sonny Lockwood*); James C. Eagles (*Tommy Tucker*); Shirley Grey (*Winnie Lloyd*); Bradley Page (*Jack Ruby* [*crook*]); Walter Walker (*Pop Lockwood* [*crook*]); Berton Churchill (*Toledo Jones* [*crook*]); Donald Kerr (*Steve Wells* [*hotel*]); Nydia Westman (*Sue Wells* [*hotel*]); Cecil Cunningham (*Mrs Chadman* [*crook*]); Thomas Jackson (*Lynch* [*crook*]); Allen Wood (*Pepper Murphy* [*crook*]); Rita La Roy (*Elsie*) [*crook*]); Clarence Muse (*Sam*).

SYNOPSIS

A group of people gather at the Luray Springs Hotel to bet on a

With Sidney Blackmer.

single race, the Capitol Handicap. The hotel roster includes Colly Tanner who has come to find her old sweetheart, Cuff Billings. Colly once deserted Billings to marry a wealthy Bostonian. Billings answers her plea for $10,000 with an offer to bet that amount against herself. When Colly's horse, *Sir Rapid,* places third, she goes to Billings to pay her bet. He insists, however, that she has won. Colly then admits to Billings that she divorced her husband and wants to stay with him.

REVIEWS

Mordaunt Hall,
The New York Times, March 18, 1933:
"Another offspring of *Grand Hotel* is now on exhibition at the Rialto. . . . It is not as ambitious a picture as *Grand Hotel,* but it is interesting. There are some impressive scenes of throngs at the race-track, of the horses in the handicap and latterly of the killing of the crook.

Carole Lombard serves this film well as the bookmaker's girl, who after a fling at marriage returns to one of her previous loves."

Variety, March 21, 1933:
"Miss Lombard gets nowhere in particular here, being the girl who, in need of coin, bets her virtue with the bookmaker against a horse she picks on the cuff."

Photoplay, April, 1933:
"A different sort of story with spice, comedy, tragedy, and Jack Oakie thrown in to provide ample good measure. One by one, the characters filter in to take rooms at a hotel near a race track. From there on the story steps out, with many a thrill and chuckle, until the death, comedy, happiness bring it to a fadeout. There's good entertainment here for nearly everybody."

Supernatural

Paramount / 1933

Directed by Victor Halperin. Screenplay by Harvey Thew and Brian Marlow. Based on the story and adaptation by Garnett Weston. Photographed by Arthur Martinelli. Dialogue director, Sidney Salkow. Running time, 64½ minutes. Released May 12, 1933.

CAST

Carole Lombard (*Roma Courtney*); Randolph Scott (*Grant Wilson*); Vivienne Osborne (*Ruth Rogen*); Alan Dinehart (*Paul Bavian*); H. B. Warner (*Dr. Houston*); Beryl Mercer (*Madame Gourjan*); William Farnum (*Robert Hammond*); Willard Robertson (*Warden*); George Burr MacAnnon (*Max*); Lyman Williams (*John Courtney*).

SYNOPSIS

In his plan to gain control of the Courtney fortune, Paul Bavian,

With Alan Dinehart.

With Randolph Scott.

a pseudo-spiritualist, notifies Roma Courtney that he has communicated with her dead brother, John. At a seance arranged by Bavian a plastocene mask of John's face is skilfully used to represent the spirit of Roma's deceased brother. During the seance Bavian makes it appear that John was murdered by Nick Hammond, Roma's guardian. Upset by what she has seen and heard, Roma leaves.

Dr. Houston, a psychologist, believes that the spirit of a deceased criminal may enter the body of a living person and continue to commit crimes. Houston confers with Ruth Rogen, the imprisoned

With Randolph Scott.

With H. B. Warner and Randolph Scott.

[107]

"Greenwich Village love-murderess," who is soon to be executed for her crimes. Ruth gives Dr. Houston permission to perform experiments on her body after her death. Ruth hopes that her spirit will seek its revenge on Bavian, the man who betrayed her to the police.

When Hammond is murdered by Bavian at a second seance, Ruth's spirit enters Roma's body. Having adopted Ruth's personality and behavior, Roma lures Bavian aboard her yacht and attempts to strangle him. John Courtney's spirit, speaking through the stricken Dr. Houston, communicates to Grant Wilson the whereabouts of Roma and Bavian. Wilson's arrival prevents Roma from killing Bavian. Bavian flees from the cabin. Up on deck he becomes caught in the halyard and is strangled to death. Having achieved its revenge, Ruth's spirit leaves Roma, who then is reunited with Wilson.

REVIEWS

Mordaunt Hall,
The New York Times, April 22, 1933:
"Notwithstanding the incredibility of many of its main incidents, *Supernatural* . . . succeeds in awakening no little interest in its spooky doings. It not only depicts the various tricks of a charlatan spiritualist but also undertakes through camera wizardry to show the spirit of a dead murderess entering the body of a wholesome girl and causing her to behave like a savage. . . . Miss Lombard's portrayal . . . is praiseworthy."

Motion Picture Herald, April 29, 1933:
"If the so-called supernatural were made rather less inconceivable, less obviously a machination than a manifestation of something beyond ordinary ken, it doubtless would have more entertainment value. Such comment may well be registered with respect to Paramount's *Supernatural.* The too obvious effort to appear mystical, mysterious and weird causes it at times to descend of its own weight to something approaching absurdity."

With Randolph Scott, William Farnum, H. B. Warner, and Alan Dinehart.

With Fredric March.

The Eagle and the Hawk

Paramount / 1933

Directed by Stuart Walker. Screenplay by Bogart Rogers and Seton I. Miller. Based on the story by John Monk Saunders. Photographed by Harry Fishbeck. Running time, 72 minutes. Released May 19, 1933.

CAST

Fredric March (*Jeremiah Young*); Cary Grant (*Henry Crocker*); Jack Oakie (*Mike Richards*); Carole Lombard (*The Beautiful Lady*); Sir Guy Standing (*Major Dunham*); Forrester Harvey (*Hogan*); Kenneth Howell (*John Stevens*); Leland Hodgson (*Kingsford*); Virginia Hammond (*Lady Erskine*); Crawfurd Kent (*General*); Douglas Scott (*Tommy*); Robert Manning (*Major Kruppman*); Adrienne D'Ambincourt (*Fanny*); Jacques Jon-Terville (*French General's aide*); Russell Scott (*Flight Sergeant*); Paul Cremonesi (*French General*); Yorke Sherwood (*Taxi driver*).

SYNOPSIS

Young, Crocker and Richards are serving in the British Flying Corps during the First World War. Crocker and Young are bitter enemies, Crocker believing that Young has conspired to keep him away from the front.

After five of his flying companions are killed, Young begins to show signs of mental strain. When the adventure-seeking Crocker reports to the front, he is assigned to Young's aircraft as observer. Although antagonists, the two men make an effective flying team. It is not long, however, before Young, who has grown more cynical about the war, is ordered to take a ten-day leave.

In London Young finds drawing room chatter about the war

With Cary Grant and Fredric March.

[109]

irritating and seeks the companionship of a beautiful woman with whom he spends the night.

Upon his return to the front, Young learns that the good-natured Richards has been killed while flying with Crocker on a needless mission. Later, Young succeeds in shooting down the notorious German ace, *Greentail*. Young's bitterness is accentuated, however, when he discovers that the German flyer was only a boy. His companions celebrate the kill. but Young delivers a passionate speech against war. Retiring to his quarters, Young commits suicide. Crocker, who really seems to have appreciated Young, is determined to erase the stigma of suicide. Taking the body up in his plane, Crocker riddles the corpse with bullets to create the impression that Young died in combat.

In the final scene, Crocker appears at Young's grave but is advised by a policeman to move along.

REVIEWS

Mordaunt Hall,
The New York Times, May 13, 1933:
"In *The Eagle and the Hawk* . . . John Monk Saunders has written a vivid and impressive account of the effect of battles in the clouds upon an American ace. It is, fortunately, devoid of the stereotyped ideas which have weakened most of such narratives. Here is a drama told with a praiseworthy sense of realism, and the leading role is portrayed very efficiently by Fredric March . . . The girl who meets him and who is impersonated by Carole Lombard does not appear until the picture is halfway through, and after a sequence that takes place in London she is not heard from again."

Variety, May 16, 1933:
"Yarn is adroitly told in both dialog and action, Jack Oakie contributing some sorely-needed comedy touches here and there. It is the only relief save for a delightfully played scene between Oakie and Adrienne D'Ambicourt, who makes the most of her single scene. Carole Lombard contributes little in spite of sincere playing."

With Fredric March.

Fredric March, Sir Guy Standing, and Cary Grant.

Brief Moment

Columbia / 1933

Directed by David Burton. Screenplay by Brian Maslow and Edith Fitzgerald. From the play by S. N. Behrman. Photographed by Ted Tetzlaff. Film editor, Gene Havlick. Assistant director, Wilbur McGough. Sound recorder, Glenn Rominger. Running time, 69 minutes. Released September 8, 1933.

CAST

Carole Lombard (*Abby Fane*); Gene Raymond (*Rodney Deane*); Monroe Owsley (*Harold Sigrift*); Donald Cook (*Franklin Deane*); Arthur Hohl (*Steve Walsh*); Reginald Mason (*Mr. Deane*); Jameson Thomas (*Count Armand*); Theresa Maxwell Conover (*Mrs. Deane*); Florence Britton (*Kay Deane*); Irene Ware (*Joan*); Herbert Evans (*Alfred*).

SYNOPSIS

Singer Abby Fane works in a nightclub owned by Steve Walsh. Rodney Deane, a rich and irresponsible playboy, falls in love and

With Gene Raymond and Monroe Owsley.

marries Abby. She tries to encourage Deane to earn a living, but he prefers to remain financially dependent on his father.

In desperation Abby goes to Deane's father and requests that he cut off her husband's income. Young Deane is given a job in his father's firm, but when Abby learns that he is spending more time at the race track than at his desk, she leaves him and returns to her job at the club.

After Abby's departure Deane changes his name and finds a real job. Later, Abby and her husband are reunited by Walsh.

REVIEWS

Film Daily, August 31, 1933:
"Carole Lombard registers strong as [the] torch singer in [an] appealing society drama. [It is] sophisticated entertainment that will appeal to the masses and prove thoroughly satisfying . . . colorfully set against a background of lavishly furnished apartments, glittering night clubs and luxurious settings."

Mordaunt Hall,
The New York Times, September 30, 1933:
"Miss Lombard and Mr. Raymond treat it as though it were entirely new. An audience cannot help being lured into a favorable reaction."

Motion Picture Herald, October 17, 1933:
"A drama rather more of the marital variety, and concentrating on the time-honored wealthy boy and cabaret girl theme, *Brief Moment* has its moments, but in the main it is not more than average entertainment, somewhat lacking in action and punch. . . . The cast is good, and the leading names make for presentable marquee material. Carole Lombard and Gene Raymond share the top of the bill, assisted by Monroe Owsley, Donald Cook and Arthur Hohl."

With Gene Raymond.

With Kent Taylor and Charles Laughton.

White Woman

Paramount / 1933

Directed by Stuart Walker. Screenplay by Samuel Hoffenstein and Gladys Lehman. Based on the story by Norman Reilly Raine and Frank Butler. Photographed by Harry Fischbeck. Songs: "Yes, My Dear," and "A Gentleman and a Scholar," written for Miss Lombard by Harry Revel and Mack Gordon. Art directors, Hans Drier and Harry Oliver. Running time, 60 minutes. Released November 10, 1933.

CAST

Charles Laughton (*Horace Prin*); Carole Lombard (*Judith Denning*); Charles Bickford (*Ballister*); Kent Taylor (*David von Eltz*); Percy Killbride (*Jakey*); Charles B. Middleton (*Fenton*); James Bell (*Hambley*); Claude King (*Chisholm*); Ethel Griffies (*Mrs. Chisholm*); Jimmie Dime (*Vaegi*); Marc Lawrence (*Connors*); Mabel Johnson (*Native chief no. 1*); Gregg Whitespear (*Native chief no. 2*).

With Kent Taylor and Charles Laughton.

[113]

With Charles Bickford.

With Charles Laughton.

SYNOPSIS

Horace Prin, the cruel overseer of a rubber plantation in Malaya, marries Judith Denning, an entertainer, who is about to be deported. Judith's life at the plantation is made tolerable by the presence of David von Eltz, one of Prin's workers. Insanely jealous, Prin tries to eliminate von Eltz, whom he considers a coward, by sending him to a region of the jungle known to be inhabited by headhunters. Von Eltz, however, proves his courage and returns to Prin's camp.

In the midst of a native uprising, Ballister, an escaped convict who has come to work for Prin, helps Judith and von Eltz make their way to the coast and safety. Having resigned themselves to death, Ballister and Prin sit down to play a last game of poker. But just as Prin, the "King of the River," draws a royal flush, his opponent is speared to death. Prin continues with the game, angry that Ballister did not live long enough to see his cards. A moment later Prin is struck dead.

REVIEWS

The New York Times, November 18, 1933:
"Having made his reputation as a wit and poet, Samuel Hoffenstein, with the blessing of the cinema califs, was put to work on a scenario of the Malay gin-and-heat genre. . . . Despite the helpful presence of Charles Laughton, *White Woman* is as original as a happy ending and as close to life as a love story in a confessions magazine.

"The appearance of Carole Lombard is the signal for the plot to go to work on those elemental emotions which the grim and embittered scenario writers are always locating in Malay."

Newsweek, November 25, 1933:
"With invaluable assistancef rom the versatile Charles Laughton, Paramount has made an interesting picture out of *Hangman's Whip,* one of last season's worst plays."

Bolero

Paramount / 1934

Directed by Wesley Ruggles. Screenplay by Horace Jackson. Based on a story by Carey Wilson and Kubec Glasmon from an idea by Ruth Ridenour. Photographed by Leo Tover. Music by Ralph Rainger. The composition, "Bolero," by Maurice Ravel. Film editor, Hugh Bennett. Sound recorder, Earl Hayman. Running time, 71 minutes. Released February 23, 1934.

CAST

George Raft (*Raoul De Baere*); Carole Lombard (*Helen Hathaway*); William Frawley (*Michael De Baere*); Frances Drake (*Leona*); Sally Rand (*Annette*); Ray Milland (*Lord Coray*); Gloria Shea (*Lucy*); Gertrude Michael (*Lady D'Argon*); Del Henderson (*Theatre manager*); Frank G. Dunn (*Hotel manager*); Martha Baumattie (*Belgian landlady*); Paul Panzer (*Bailiff*); Adolph Milar (*German manager [beer garden]*); Anne Shaw (*Young matron*); Phyllis Smalley (*Leona's angel*); John Irwin (*Porter*); Gregory Golubeff (*Orchestra leader*).

SYNOPSIS

Raoul De Baere, determined to become a famous dancer, rises from cheap music hall and beer garden performances to the ownership of a swank night club in Paris. Experience has taught the ambitious Raoul that he can best achieve success by maintaining a purely business relationship with his female dancing partners.

In Europe, Raoul meets Helen who admits at the outset that she is only interested in him professionally. By becoming Raoul's partner Helen hopes that she will have a better opportunity of marrying a rich husband.

The dancing act of Raoul and Helen is a huge success. It is not long, however, before Raoul, normally abrupt and businesslike, develops an affection for Helen. She finds the dancer attractive, but has become fond of Lord Coray who is very much in love with Helen.

On the night Raoul and Helen are to perform the "Bolero," France enters the First World War. Helen listens with pride as Raoul tells the fashionable audience that he intends to enlist the next day. Later, backstage, he cynically confesses that his enlistment is only intended to publicize the night club and attract business when the war is over. Upset by this revelation, Helen leaves him to marry Lord Coray.

When the war is over in 1918, Raoul returns with a weakened heart. He is determined, however, to reopen his club and perform

With George Raft.

With George Raft.

the Bolero. He chooses Annette, a dancer he knew before the war, to become his new partner. When Annette becomes intoxicated on opening night, Helen, who is seated in the audience with Lord Coray, agrees to substitute. Raoul and Helen, dancing atop an enormous drum, give a brilliant performance of Ravel's "Bolero." Having been wildly applauded, the exhausted Raoul suffers a fatal heart attack in his dressingroom. His dying words are spoken to Helen: "I'm too good for this joint."

REVIEWS

The New York Times, February 17, 1934:
"The exterior attractiveness which Mr. Raft brings to the role gives *Bolero* considerable color . . . and the film, without coming close to realizing the real possibilities of the story as an overpowering study of megalomania, does manage to be moderately entertaining. *Bolero* is also helped by the [performance] . . . of Carole Lombard, as the dance partner who turns out to be equally hard-boiled about romance and finally marries a member of the British peerage."

Film Daily, February 17, 1934:
"Against a stirring background of Ravel's 'Bolero,' which is utilized judiciously and never overdone, an attractive and generally entertaining production has been fashioned. Because of its theme, dealing with an ambitious dancer, played by George Raft, and his women partners, the picture's appeal is likely to be stronger in the feminine field, but this doesn't mean it hasn't plenty of things to interest the man as well."

Motion Picture Herald, February 17, 1934:
"Production settings and groupings in the second half of the picture are lavish and striking. These are helpful in consolidating the interest created in the opening identifying sequences. . . . The picture has lots of novelty in both story and presentation."

George Raft,
The Saturday Evening Post, January 24, 1948:
"Since the release of *Bolero* many pictures have featured dancing. But because this was the first one to do it, because it was built around a man I admired, and because it gave me a chance to dance again, the role always will be a favorite with me."

We're Not Dressing

Paramount / 1934

Directed by Norman Taurog. Screenplay by Horace Jackson, Francis
Martin, and George Marion, Jr. Based on the story by Benjamin
Glazer. Photographed by Charles Lang. Music and lyrics by Harry
Revel and Mack Gordon. Songs: "Love Thy Neighbor," "Good
Night, Lovely Lady," "May I?" "She Reminds Me of You," "Once
in a Blue Moon," "It's a New Spanish Custom." Film editor,
Stuart Heisler. Art direction, Hans Drier and Ernst Fegte. Running
time, 74 minutes. Released April 27, 1934.

CAST

Bing Crosby (*Stephen Jones*); Carole Lombard (*Doris Worthington*); George Burns (*George*); Gracie Allen (*Gracie*); Ethel Merman (*Edith*); Leon Errol (*Hubert*); Jay Henry (*Prince Alexander Stofani*); Ray Milland (*Prince Michael Stofani*); John Irwin
(*Old sailor*); Charles Morris (*Captain*); Ben Hendricks (*First
ship's officer*); Ted Oliver (*Second ship's officer*).

SYNOPSIS

The Princes Alexander and Michael Stofani along with Hubert
and his fiancée, Edith, join wealthy Doris Worthington on her
yacht for a cruise in the South Pacific. Aboard the yacht is Stephen
Jones, a deck hand, who has the responsibility of exercising Doris'
pet bear.

When Hubert takes the helm the yacht is wrecked. All members
of the crew are lost except Jones, who swims to an island with the

With Bing Crosby.

they must work if they expect to eat. Jones, all the while, is very much in love with Doris, an affection which is reciprocated.

On another part of the island are two botanists, George (Burns) and Gracie (Allen). Gracie, who believes flora and fauna are a vaudeville team, occupies herself with setting animal traps of fantastic invention.

When the rescue ships arrive, Jones believes that Doris is making fun of his serious attentions. They board different vessels, but when Doris transfers to his ship, Jones is convinced that she loves him.

REVIEWS

Mordaunt Hall,
The New York Times, April 26, 1934:
"It has all the plausibility and romantic flavor of the average musical comedy. It is nicely photographed and cleverly directed, the sort of thing that, while it may have too many moaning melodies is invariably diverting... Miss Lombard is attractive and competent."

The Literary Digest, May 12, 1934:
"Based not too exactly on Sir James M. Barrie's *The Admirable Crichton,* it recounts, in a broadly farcical manner, the rise of a menial to leader during the shipwreck of a yacht. It devolves upon Bing Crosby, radio crooner, to play and sing the central role and he does his task excellently.... Carole Lombard, as the boatowner who suddenly finds her fate in the hands of the sailor she had discharged and then falls in love with him, is not so successful in keeping the piece madly hilarious, but this is admirably accomplished by the supporting comics in the cast, particularly Burns and Allen, Ethel Merman and Leon Errol."

Twentieth Century

Columbia / 1934

Directed by Howard Hawks. Story and screenplay by Ben Hecht and Charles MacArthur. Photographed by Joseph August. Film editor, Gene Havlick. Assistant director, C. C. Coleman. Sound recorder, Edward Bernds. Running time, 84 minutes. Released May 11, 1934.

CAST

John Barrymore (*Oscar Jaffe*); Carole Lombard (*Lily Garland*); Walter Connolly (*Oliver Webb*); Roscoe Karns (*Owen O'Malley*); Charlie Levison (*Max Jacobs*); Etienne Girardot (*Clark*); Dale Fuller (*Sadie*); Ralph Forbes (*George Smith*); Billie Seward (*Anita*); Clifford Thompson (*Lockwood*); James P. Burtis (*Conductor*); Gigi Parrish (*Myrtle Schultz*); Edgar Kennedy (*Mr. McGonigle*); Ed Gargan (*Sheriff*); Snowflake (*Porter*); Herman Bing (*First beard*); Lee Kohlmer (*Second beard*); Pat Flaherty (*Flannigan*).

SYNOPSIS

Under the tutelage of Oscar Jaffe, an eccentric Broadway impresario, Lily Garland, formerly Mildred Plotka, a department store clerk, becomes a great actress, acclaimed by audiences and critics. For three years Lily is Jaffe's personal property, his star actress and mistress. Their association is punctuated by moments of anger and reconciliation. After one such argument, Lily decides to

With director Howard Hawks and John Barrymore.

With Charles Lane, Walter Connolly, Roscoe Karns, and John Barrymore.

[119]

With John Barrymore.

leave Jaffe. Independently, she pursues a motion picture career in Hollywood.

Oscar Jaffe experiences financial and professional failure following Lily's departure. Accompanied by Oliver Webb and Owen O'Malley, his manager and press agent respectively, Jaffe eludes his creditors in Chicago by boarding the Twentieth Century Limited for New York. On board the express train he learns that Lily and her fiancée, George Smith, a football hero whom Jaffe detests, are also passengers. As the Limited speeds to New York, Jaffe hopes to reestablish his position and credit by persuading Lily to appear in his production of *The Passion Play*. Jaffe and Garland engage in a riotous verbal exchange, a mixture of shouting and soft sweetness, orchestrated by the stomping of feet and the slamming of compartment doors. Further comic relief is provided by two bearded gentlemen who hope to be cast in Jaffe's play, and a religious fanatic who has delusions of great wealth. By the time the Limited has reached New York, Jaffe has tricked Lily into signing a contract.

REVIEWS

Mordaunt Hall,
The New York Times, May 4, 1934:
"Carole Lombard gives an able portrayal as Lily."

Variety, May 8, 1934:
"Miss Lombard, looking very well, must take Barrymore's abuse as his mistress and hand-made star for the first hundred feet, but when she goes temperamental she's permitted to do some head-to-head temperament punching with him."

William Fleming, *Shadowplay,* June, 1934:
"...that's the sort of picture it was, with Lombard like no other Lombard you've seen.... When you see her, you'll forget the rather restrained and somewhat stilted Lombard of old. You'll see a star

With John Barrymore.

*With Ralph Forbes and
Roscoe Karns.*

blaze out of this scene and that scene, high spots Carole never
dreamed of hitting."

Photoplay, July, 1934:
"John Barrymore's endless versatility, Carole Lombard's fiery talent
which few suspected she had, and Walter Connolly's customarily
good performance pack the laughs into this film. It is broad farce
with a veneer of satire, moving at a dizzy pace."

London Times, July 9, 1934:
"*Twentieth Century*...once again proves that Hollywood has a
decided gift for satire, and Mr. John Barrymore gives an excellent
caricature of an actor in the old romantic tradition."

*With Roscoe Karns, John Barrymore, and
Walter Connolly.*

*Roscoe Karns, John Barrymore,
and Walter Connolly.*

Now and Forever

Paramount / 1934

Directed by Henry Hathaway. Produced by Louis D. Lighton. Screenplay by Vincent Lawrence and Sylvia Thalliery. Adapted from the story by Jack Kirkland and Melville Baker. Photographed by Henry Fischbeck. Music and lyrics by Harry Revel and Mack Gordon. Art directon, Hans Dreier and Robert Usher. Sound recorder, Harold Lewis. Running time, 00 minutes. Released August 31, 1934.

CAST

Gary Cooper (*Jerry Day*); Carole Lombard (*Toni Carstairs*); Shirley Temple (*Penelope Day*); Sir Guy Standing (*Felix Evans*); Charlotte Granville (*Mrs. J. H. P. Crane*); Gilbert Emery (*James*

With Shirley Temple.

With Gary Cooper, Shirley Temple, and Charlotte Granville.

[122]

*With Gary Cooper and
Shirley Temple.*

Higginson); Henry Kolker (*Mr. Clark*); Tetsu Komal (*Mr. Ling*);
Jameson Thomas (*Chris Carstairs*); Harry Stubbe (*Mr. O'Neill*);
Egon Brecker (*Doctor*).

SYNOPSIS

Jerry Day, an international crook, and his partner Toni Carstairs,
go their separate ways following a swindle in Shanghai. Day returns
to America, intending to sell the custody of his little daughter,
Penelope, to wealthy James Higginson, his former brother-in-law.
At the Higginson estate, however, Day is so touched by the child
that he decides to reclaim her.

With Gary Cooper.

*With Shirley Temple and
Gary Cooper.*

[123]

After swindling another crook, Felix Evans, Day and Penelope sail to Europe. Reunited in Paris, Day and Toni try to establish a home for Penelope. Day, however, returns to thievery when he fails in his attempt to earn an honest living selling real estate.

Evans, who is also in Europe, persuades Day to steal a necklace belonging to Mrs. J. H. P. Crane, a society matron who has befriended Penelope. While Mrs. Crane entertains Penelope at a birthday party, Day steals the necklace. Having violated the "honor bright" compact with his daughter, Day decides to recover the gems which are now in Evans' possession. Day shoots Evans in self-defense and returns the necklace to Mrs. Crane. Wounded in the exchange of fire with Evans, Day secures Mrs. Crane's promise to adopt Penelope. After the departure of Penelope and Mrs. Crane, Day collapses from his bullet wound. Regaining consciousness at the hospital, Day realizes that he will be punished, but Toni assures him that "Penny" will understand.

REVIEWS

André Sennwald,
The New York Times, October 13, 1934:
"The photoplay is visually handsome and it is attractively played by Mr. Cooper and Miss Lombard. With Shirley's assistance it becomes, despite its violent assaults upon the spectator's credulity, a pleasant enough entertainment."

Photoplay, October, 1934:
"Gary [Cooper] is a life-loving vagabond adventurer, unhampered by scruples about honesty. Shirley [Temple] is his motherless tot, and Carole Lombard is the woman who can't help loving him in spite of his faults. His regeneration, through them, is the theme—presented interestingly, and moving through colorful locales."

With Gary Cooper.

With Charlotte Granville and Shirley Temple.

With Roger Pryor.

Lady By Choice

A Robert North Production / 1934

Released through Columbia pictures. Directed by David Burton. Screenplay by Jo Swerling. Based on a story by Dwight Taylor. Photographed by Ted Tetzlaff. Film editor, Viola Lawrence. Assistant director, Arthur Black. Sound recorder, Glenn Rominger. Running time, 74 minutes. Released, October 15, 1934.

CAST

Carole Lombard (*Alabam' Lee*); May Robson (*Patricia Patterson* [*Patsy*]); Roger Pryor (*Johnny Mills*); Walter Connolly (*Judge Daly*); Arthur Hohl (*Kendall*); Raymond Walburn (*Front O'Malley*); James Burke (*Brannigan*); Mariska Aldrich (*Lucretia*); John Doyle (*Walsh*); Henry Kolker (*Opper*); Lillian Harmer (*Miss Kingsley*); Abe Denovitch (*Louie*); Fred (Snowflake) Toone (*Mose*).

SYNOPSIS

Patsy, a genial alcoholic, is brought before the night court of Judge Daly following her arrest for breaking up a saloon. Johnny Mills, the son of one of Patsy's old boyfriends, persuades Judge Daly to

With Arthur Hohl and Roger Pryor.

parole the alcoholic to a retirement home for ladies. Also in court is Alabam' Lee, a fan dancer, who has been arrested because of her performance.

When Mother's Day approaches, Alabam's press agent, Front O'Malley, suggests that she publicize her dancing act by "adopting" a mother. On a visit to the retirement home, Alabam' sees Patsy and "adopts" her.

The adopted mother takes her new role seriously. In an effort to help her "daughter" professionally, Patsy hires instructors in drama, voice, and dance. She supervises Alabam's personal life by encouraging a romance with Johnny Mills.

For a time it appears that Alabam' is only interested in Mills because of his inheritance. When Alabam' learns that Mills will be disinherited should he marry her, she returns to her old job as a fan dancer. Patsy, however, prevents Alabam's performance by having the cabaret raided. Appearing before Judge Daly, Alabam' is given the choice of one year in jail or marriage to Mills. Alabam' chooses Mills.

REVIEWS

The New York Times, November 17, 1934:
"*Lady By Choice* is . . . a well-rounded story, enacted by a tried and true cast, directed with sureness by David Burton and spiced with Jo Swerling's natural robust and clever dialogue."

Variety, November 20, 1934:
"Carole Lombard does a lot for the picture. She is forceful, vibrant, and once or twice she shows far greater power than in her previous work."

Photoplay, December, 1934:
"Ring up another one for the miraculous May Robson . . . Carole Lombard runs up a score of her own as the disillusioned fan dancer who adopts a 'mother' from the Old Ladies' Home as a publicity gag."

With May Robson and Raymond Walburn.

With Chester Morris.

The Gay Bride

Metro-Goldwyn-Mayer / 1934

Directed by Jack Conway. Produced by John W. Considine, Jr. Screenplay by Bella and Samuel Spewack. Based on the *Saturday Evening Post* story, "Repeal," by Charles Francis Coe. Photographed by Ray June. Music by Jack Virgil. Film editor, Frank Sullivan. Art direction, Cedric Gibbons. Associate art directors, Stan Rogers and Edwin B. Willis. Costumes by Dolly Tree. Sound recorder, Douglas Shearer. Running time, 82 minutes. Released December 14, 1934.

CAST

Carole Lombard (*Mary*); Chester Morris (*Office boy*); ZaSu Pitts (*Mirabelle*); Leo Carrillo (*Mickey*); Nat Pendleton (*Shoots Magiz*); Sam Hardy (*Dingle*); Walter Walker (*MacPherson*).

SYNOPSIS

Ambitious for wealth, Mary makes friends with Shoots Magiz, an underworld figure who is producing a show in which she appears. Mary finds Shoots insufferable but marries him for his money. When Shoots is murdered by Dingle, Mary's life is further complicated. Dingle in turn is eliminated by Mickey. In the end the gangster's widow reforms and marries the office boy.

With Chester Morris and Nat Pendleton.

REVIEWS

Variety, December 18, 1934:
"Gangster pictures are gone, and this one won't do anything to bring them back. It'll do more to consign their permanently to Davey Jones' locker down where grosses don't count. It deals with hoodlums in a post-prohibition era, but fails to freshen up the story and the conventional means taken to carry it out. . . . Morris and Miss Lombard are handicapped by both parts and dialog, while Zasu Pitts and Leo Carillo, among supporters, go nowhere."

New York Times, December 19, 1934:
"Although the Rialto's new film is probably pretty small pertaters according to the lofty standards of the academicians, it provides some unusually loud and vigorous laughter at the expense of the professional assassins of the underworld. . . . Carole Lombard enacts the role of the starry-eyed lady with a comic gravity which is decidedly effective."

Photoplay, January, 1935:
"A good story loaded with plot complications and blurry character drawings. Even Zasu Pitts seems more bewildered than usual."

With ZaSu Pitts.

With George Raft.

Rumba

Paramount / 1935

Directed by Marion Gering. Screenplay by Howard J. Green. Additional dialogue by Harry Ruskin and Frank Partas. Adapted from the story by Guy Endore and Seena Owen. Photgraphed by Ted Tetzlaff. Music and lyrics by Ralph Rainger. Spanish lyrics by François B. deValdes. Dances and ensembles by Veloz and Yolanda. Miss Lombard's and Mr. Raft's specialty dance by Veloz and Yolanda. Film editor, Hugh Bennett. Art direction, Hans Dreier and Robert Usher. Costumes by Travis Banton. Sound recorder, J. A. Goodrich. Running time, 70 minutes. Released February 8, 1935.

CAST

George Raft (*Joe Martin*); Carole Lombard (*Diana Harrison*); Lynne Overman (*Flash*); Margo (*Carmelita*); Monroe Owsley (*Hobart Fletcher*); Iris Adrian (*Goldie Allen*); Samuel S. Hinds (*Henry B. Harrison*); Virginia Hammond (*Mrs. Harrison*); Gail Patrick (*Patsy*); James Thomas (*Solanger*); Soledad Jiminez (*Maria*); Paul Porcasi (*Carlos*); Raymond McKee (*Dance director*); Akim Tamiroff (*Tony*); Eldred Tidbury (*Watkins*).

SYNOPSIS

Joe Martin is similar to Raoul in *Bolero,* a brilliant dancer, tough and ambitious. When wealthy Diana Harrison, vacationing in Cuba, first meets Martin, she appears to dislike him. Later, after Diana sees him dance in a Havana night club, she finds him more attractive. But Martin misunderstands her intentions and a fight breaks

With George Raft.

With George Raft.

out between Fletcher, Diana's escort, and the dancer. When order is restored, Martin loses his job, but not his ambition.

He journeys to the interior and sees a native performance of the rumba. As a result, Martin is inspired to open his own night club and perform the rumba with Carmelita, his Cuban girlfriend.

When the new club opens, Diana is impressed by Martin's dancing and offers to finance his act in New York. The dancer, however, receives a mysterious warning that it will be dangerous for him to go to New York. Martin is told that a gunman there believes that he betrayed his gangland compatriot to the police.

The New York newspapers warn of the possible danger that awaits Martin should he perform at Solanger's Club. On opening night every table is filled. Carmelita, however, can no longer endure the tension and collapses. Martin is prepared to give a solo performance but Diana, fearful that he will be an easy target, volunteers to be his partner.

Later, it is learned that Flash, the dancer's associate, invented the idea of an assassination attempt in order to publicize Martin's New York debut.

REVIEWS

Variety, February 27, 1935:
"An attractive title and some fascinating studio work behind it are what *Rumba* has chiefly to offer. It's a good looking production that doesn't rate high in a literary way, but has managed to capture quite a lot of the spirit of the dance for which it is named. It listens and looks like a better than moderate grosser."

Photoplay, April, 1935:
"*Rumba*" has a less interesting story than *Bolero*. Raft again is a dancer. Carole, a wealthy society girl, falls for him. They seem to misunderstand each other until the very end."

With Gail Patrick.

With Fred MacMurray and Albert Conti.

Hands Across the Table

Paramount / 1935

Directed by Mitchell Leisen. Produced by E. Lloyd Sheldon. Supervised by Ernst Lubitsch. Screenplay by Norman Krasna, Vincent Laurence, and Herbert Fields. Based on a story by Vina Delmar. Photographed by Ted Tetzlaff. Music and lyrics by Sam Caslow and Frederick Hollander. Running time, 80 minutes. Released October 18, 1935.

CAST

Carole Lombard (*Regi Allen*); Fred MacMurray (*Theodore Drew III*); Ralph Bellamy (*Allen Macklyn*); Astrid Allwyn (*Vivian Snowden*); Ruth Donnelly (*Laura*); Marie Prevost (*Nona*); Joseph Tozer (*Peter*); William Demarest (*Natty*); Edward Gargan (*Pinky Kelly*); Ferdinand Munier (*Miles*); Harold Minjir (*Valentine*); Marcelle Corday (*French maid*).

With Fred MacMurray.

[131]

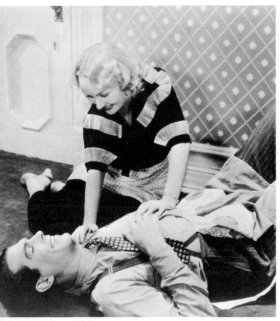

With Fred MacMurray.

With Ralph Bellamy.

SYNOPSIS

Cynical about love and resolved to marry for money, Regi Allen, a young manicurist, is at first attracted to wealthy Allen Macklyn. Macklyn, a cripple, is fascinated by Regi and intends to propose to her.

Theodore Drew III, an impoverished playboy who is preparing to marry wealthy Vivian Snowden, comes into the barbershop one day for a manicure. Believing that he is rich, Regi eagerly accepts his invitation to dinner. Drew entertains Regi in grand style, spending the money which Vivian gave him for a trip to Bermuda while the Snowdens prepared for an elaborate wedding. Too intoxicated to make his travel connections, Drew is forced to spend the night in Regi's apartment. When the manicurist returns from work the next day, the playboy confesses that he is penniless. "How could the Drews be broke?" Regi inquires. "Maybe you, uh, heard about the Big Crash? Well that was, uh, us," Drew replies.

Regi allows Drew to spend his Bermuda vacation in her flat on 120th Street. Regi and Drew gradually discard their cynical ideas about marriage and fall in love. Drew breaks his engagement with Vivian while Macklyn is denied an opportunity to propose to Regi. Flipping a coin, Drew promises to marry Regi after he has found a job.

REVIEWS

Otis Ferguson,
The New Republic, November 13, 1935:
"The trouble and the danger with light comedy as a rule is that it is self-conscious over its lack of weight and either leaves reality altogether in an attempt to be capricious and unexpected about everything, or fastens on each excuse for feeling with a hollow and forced semblance of deep emotion. That *Hands Across the Table* keeps the delicate and hard balance between these two courses of procedure is partly the work of direction, cutting, dialogue writing; but considerably the work of Carole Lombard and Fred MacMurray."

London Times, November 25, 1935:
"It is a fashion among many of the pseudo-intellectuals of the cinema to decry completely the machine-made quality of the American film; to scorn the wisecrack; and to condemn offhand as insincere anything that savours of sophistication. Yet without the help of these so-called vices such films as *Hands Across the Table* could hardly be made. That would be a singular misfortune, for a comedy such as this has moments of real brilliance. Mr. Mitchell Leisen, the director, knows precisely what he wants to do and wastes no time in doing it. The story is as slender as a young willow, but before the film comes to an end a bat has been made out of it which sends almost everything to the boundary.

"The whole success of the film depends on the dexterity of the dialogue, the smoothness of its sophistication, and on the ingenuity with which incident is made to follow incident. And a success it is. Mr. Leisen never comes between the actors and their audience, and the dialogue between Miss Lombard and Mr. MacMurray has the happy air of spontaneity which transforms it from the printed script into an extemporary expression of character. It is as if each phrase was only thought of the moment it was uttered. Only once is the brittle surface broken, and characters who are never meant to exist outside artificial comedy embarrassingly attempt to enter a world to which they do not belong. Otherwise the game goes on gaily, and most of the strokes are brilliant in style and played so quickly that it is difficult to detect when one leaves off and the other begins."

Photoplay, December, 1935:
"Not since *Twentieth Century* has Carole Lombard had such ample scope for her fine flair for sophisticated light comedy, punctuated by telling tenderness, as in this role of the manicurist, *Regi Allen*. A grand teammate, Fred MacMurray as the blueblood playboy with empty pockets shares performance honors with her.

John Milford,
Film Pictorial (London), March 28, 1936:
"Whenever I see a picture with a really novel and unusual story, I feel like cheering. When, on top of that, it has sparkling dialogue, fast movement and finished acting, I let go and *do* cheer. . . .

   "It is one of the brightest and best of the lighthearted comedy romances which Hollywood does so well. And here's a special cheer for Carole, who nowadays acts as beautifully as she looks."

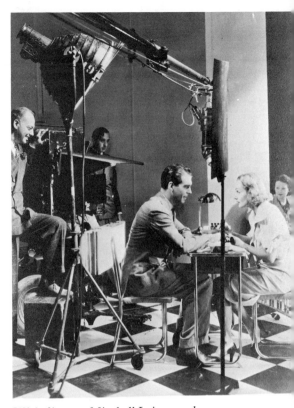

With director Mitchell Leisen and Fred MacMurray.

With Fred MacMurray.

[133]

With Cesar Romero.

Love Before Breakfast

Universal / 1936

Directed by Walter Lang. Produced by Edmund Grainger. Screenplay by Herbert Fields. Based on the novel, *Spinster Dinner*, by Faith Baldwin. Additional dialogue by Gertrude Princell. Photographed by Ted Tetzlaff. Musical director, Franz Waxman. Film editor, Maurice Wright. Assistant director, Phil Karlstein. Art direction, Albert D'Agostino. Miss Lombard's gowns by Travis Banton. Other gowns by Brymer. Sound recorder, Gilbert Kurland. Editorial supervision, Maurice Pivar. Running time, 70 minutes. Released March 9, 1936.

CAST

Carole Lombard (*Kay Colby*); Preston Foster (*Scott Miller*); Janet Beecher (*Mrs. Colby*); Cesar Romero (*Bill Wadsworth*); Betty Lawford (*Contessa Campanella*); Douglas Blackley (*College boy*); Don Briggs (*Stuart Farnum*); Bert Roach (*Fat man*); Andre Beranger (*Charles*); Richard Carle (*Brinkerhoff*); Ed Barton (*Jerry*); Diana Gibson (*Clerk*); Joyce Compton (*Mary Lee Jackson*); John King (*Johnny*); E. E. Clive (*Captain*); Forrester Harvey (*First mate*); Mia Ichioka (*Yuki*); John Rogers (*Dickson*).

SYNOPSIS

Bill Wadsworth and his boss, oilman Scott Miller, are in love with the same woman, Kay Colby. In a scheme to win Kay's affection, Miller offers Wadsworth the opportunity of working at the branch office in Japan. Wadsworth accepts, to Kay's disappointment. Miller arranges for the beautiful Contessa Campanella to sail on the same ship, hopeful that Wadsworth will succumb to her charms.

Kay seems to understand Miller's intentions. Although Miller helps her out of difficulties during Wadsworth's absence, Kay shows little affection for the rich oilman. Only after Kay receives a cable stating that Wadsworth is planning to wed Contessa does she agree

With Preston Foster.

With Ted Tetzlaff, director Walter Lang, Syd Hydeman, Cesar Romero, and Phil Karlstein on location at Wilmington Harbor, California.

to marry Miller. Just as Kay is beginning to find Miller more attractive, he has a moment of conscience and summons Wadsworth home. She breaks their engagement, angry that Miller should attempt to arrange other people's lives. Her love for Miller is rekindled, however, at a party on the oilman's yacht. After a fall overboard, Kay and Miller are married by the captain.

REVIEWS

Motion Picture Herald, February 29, 1936:
"Built upon the premise that a man and woman can't get along either with or without each other, this picture stacks up as the kind of attraction for any kind of audience. Nicely produced, set in a semi-sophisticated atmosphere, the yarn is motivated by a well-grounded series of uniquely contrived situations, which, with action and dialogue expertly blended, result in the picture stepping along at a fast pace. Wholesome, while having just enough of that ultimate romantic quality to keep interest continually pepped up, the yarn concentrates on fun."

The New York Times, March 14, 1936:
"A story thin to the point of emaciation is padded out with blatantly effective lines, boisterous incidents and scene after scene involving the stylized mouth and eyebrows of Miss Carole Lombard sufficiently to make of *Love Before Breakfast,* at the Roxy, a quantitatively passable picture."

John Milford,
Film Pictorial (London), July 25, 1936:
"The story is just a succession of squabbles and people shouting at one another, and when one character says: 'I think maybe I'll get drunk; then perhaps I shall understand what is going on around here,' he is summing up the whole picture. It's grand entertainment for those who like this type of sophisticated slapstick. Carole and Preston Foster are excellent."

With Preston Foster.

[135]

The Princess Comes Across

Paramount / 1936

Directed by William K. Howard. Produced by Arthur Hornblow, Jr. Screenplay by Walter De Leon, Francis Martin, Frank Butler, and Don Hartman. Based on the story by Philip MacDonald. Adapted from the novel by Louis Lucien Rogers. Photographed by Ted Tetzlaff. Special photographic effects by Farciot Edouart and Dewey Wrigley. Music and lyrics by Phil Boutelje and Jack Scholl. Film editor, Paul Weatherwax. Assistant director, Harry Scott. Sound recorder, Harold Lewis. Running time, 75 minutes. Released May 22, 1936.

CAST

Carole Lombard (*Princess Olga*); Fred MacMurray (*King Mantell*); Douglas Dumbrille (*Lorel*); Alison Skipworth (*Lady Gertrude Allwyn*); William Frawley (*Benton*); Porter Hall (*Darcy*);

With Fred MacMurray.

George Barbier (*Captain Nicholls*); Lumsden Hare (*Cragg*); Sig Ruman (*Steindorf*); Mischa Auer (*Morevitch*); Tetsu Komai (*Kawati*); Bradley Page (*The stranger*); Bennie Bartlet (*Ship's bellhop*).

SYNOPSIS

A Brooklyn-born showgirl assumes the disguise of Olga, a Swedish princess, in an attempt to further her career in films. Olga's girl-friend, also a showgirl, coaches her and gives general support as "Lady Gertrude Allwyn." Aboard a transatlantic liner bound for New York, Olga becomes acquainted with bandleader King Mantell and his friend Benton. During the voyage Olga is blackmailed by a man who knew her in Brooklyn. When the blackmailer is mysteriously murdered in her stateroom, Olgo persuades Mantell to remove the body to another cabin. Five foreign police agents en route to a convention attempt to solve the crime. Mantell, however, captures the killer. Having fallen in love with Olga, Mantell agrees to help the "princess" continue her masquerade. Upon her arrival in New York, however, Olga gives herself away in a radio speech.

REVIEWS

Motion Picture Herald, May 16, 1936:
"Fresh in concept, played against an atmosphere of easy gayety, its amusement quality is a worthy follow-up to *Hands Across the Table*."

Variety, June 10, 1936:
"With William K. Howard's direction accounting for a slick piece of satire and whodunit merging, and Carole Lombard and Fred MacMurray given a set of story personalities that jell, *The Princess Comes Across* spells happy tidings around the boxoffice. Even though the plot occasionally gets murky, the whole thing is managed with such crispness and lightness that the defects become hardly noticeable. Enhancing the quality of the entertainment is the skill brought to play in nimbly hopping from one mood to another without slowing up the pace of the narrative."

With Fred MacMurray, director William K. Howard, and Ted Tetzlaff.

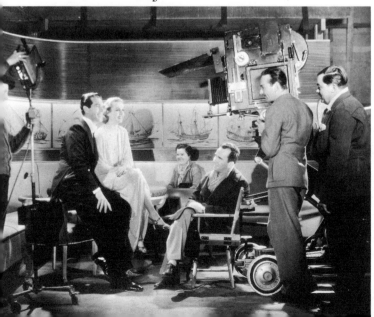

With Fred MacMurray.

On the set with Fred MacMurray.

My Man Godfrey

A Universal picture / 1936

Directed by Gregory La Cava. Screenplay by Morrie Ryskind and Eric Hatch. Based on the novel by Eric Hatch. Photographed by Ted Tetzlaff. Music by Charles Previn. Film editor, Ted Kent. Film supervisor, Maurice Pivar. Assistant director, Scott R. Beal. Art direction, Charles D. Hall. Running time, 93 minutes. Released September 6, 1936.

CAST

William Powell (*Godfrey Parke*); Carole Lombard (*Irene Bullock*); Alice Brady (*Angelica Bullock*); Gail Patrick (*Cornelia Bullock*); Jean Dixon (*Molly*); Eugene Pallette (*Alexander Bullock*); Alan Mowbray (*Tommy Gray*); Mischa Auer (*Carlo*); Robert Light (*Faithful George*) Pat Flaherty (*Mike*); Franklin Pangborn (*Master of ceremonies*); Grady Sutton (*Van Rumple*);

With William Powell, Gail Patrick, Mischa Auer, Alice Brady, Eugene Pallette, director Gregory La Cava, and Ted Tetzlaff (seated behind the camera) during the filming of My Man Godfrey.

With William Powell.

With Mischa Auer, William Powell, and director Gregory La Cava.

Ed Gargan (*Detective*); James Flavin (*Second detective*); Robert Perry (*Doorman*).

SYNOPSIS

Irene and Cornelia Bullock, participants in a scavenger hunt, must add a "forgotten man" to a list of articles that range from Japanese goldfish to tennis rackets. The two debutantes are driven to a shanty village near the East River where they discover the bearded Godfrey Parke amidst tar paper shacks and smoking debris. Offended by the nature of their mission, Godfrey angrily backs Cornelia into an ash heap. Recovering her poise, Cornelia returns to the hotel.

With William Powell and Gail Patrick

[139]

Irene remains at the dump, pleased that Godfrey has humiliated her snobbish sister. When she tells him that Cornelia will probably win the scavenger hunt, Godfrey agrees to appear at the party as Irene's "forgotten man." Upon their arrival at the hotel, Irene is judged the winner after which Godfrey delivers a short speech, criticizing the gathering. Feeling sorry for Godfrey, Irene offers him employment as the family butler.

Soon afterward, the Bullocks learn from Tommy Gray, a friend of the family, that Godfrey was his classmate at Harvard. Later, Godfrey explains to Gray that a love affair had brought him to the brink of suicide. The optimistic attitude of the unemployed at the shanty village, however, had rekindled his spirit.

The gentlemanly and intelligent Godfrey brings a measure of stabilty to the zany household of Alexander Bullock. Attired in butler's livery, he expels Mrs. Bullock's lecherous protege, Carlo; alleviates Mr. Bullock's financial distress; and teaches Cornelia a lesson in humility. Godfrey relieves the plight of the unemployed at the city dump by constructing a night club by the East River. Godfrey is deemed a suitable marriage partner for Irene when it is learned that he comes from an old Boston family.

REVIEWS

Motion Picture Herald, June 20, 1936:
"When [the audience] couldn't help but drown out ensuing laughter, it could only resort to limply sitting back in its seats and making a stern effort to gather fresh strength to give vent to pleasure in appreciation of the nonsense of the screen."

With William Powell.

With Eugene Pallette, Alice Brady, and Mischa Auer.

London Times, September 23, 1936:
"The mild bite of its by no means remorseless satire is of great assistance in the farce of which this film is largely composed. The exuberance of the idle rich is most agreeably turned into a spectacle of pure imbecility, with much charmingly inconsequent dialogue, and with a pleasing demonstration of the theory that the irresponsible possession of wealth produces characters which strongly resemble those of Chekov."

Variety, September 23, 1936:
"Miss Lombard's role is the more difficult of the two, since it calls for pressure acting all the way, and it was no simple trick to refrain from overworking the insanity plea in a many-sided assignment. It's Powell's job to be normal and breezily comic in the madcap household, and that doesn't require stretching for him."

Graham Greene,
The Spectator (London), n.d.:
"... the film, in the earlier sequences well conveys the atmosphere of an American Cherry Orchard, of a class with little of the grace and all the futility and some of the innocence of its Russian counterpart. Unfortunately to these Americans prosperity returns, there is no dignified exit while the axes thud in the orchard, only the great glossy club rising over the wilderness of empty tins, and, last muddle and bewilderment, the marriage of the reformer and the brainless 'lovely.' "

Advertisement for My Man Godfrey.

With Gail Patrick.

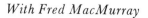
With Fred MacMurray

Swing High, Swing Low

Paramount / 1937

Directed by Mitchell Leisen. Screenplay by Virginia Van Upp and Oscar Hammerstein II. Based on the play, *Burlesque,* by George Manker Watters and Arthur Hopkins. Photographed by Ted Tetzlaff. Special photographic effects, Farciot Edouart. Musical direction, Boris Morros. Compositions and arrangements by Victor Young and Phil Boutelje. Vocal supervision, Al· Siegel. Songs: "Swing High, Swing Low," by Burton Lane and Ralph Freed;

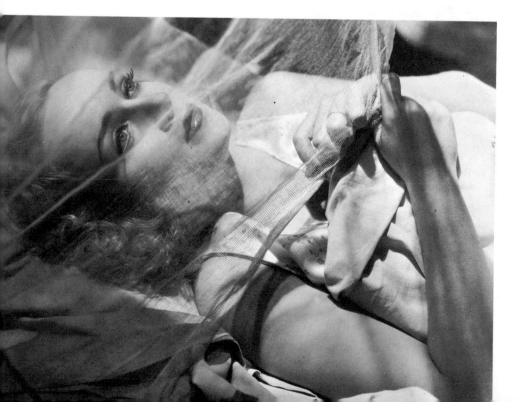

"I Hear a Call to Arms," and "Panamania" by Al Siegel and Sam Caslow; "If It Isn't Pain, Then It Isn't Love," by Ralph Rainger and Leo Robin; "Lonely Little Senorita," by Leo Robin and Julian Oliver. Film editor, Edna Warren. Assistant director, Edgar Anderson. Art direction, Hans Dreier and Ernst Fegte. Interior decorations, A. E. Freudeman. Costumes by Travis Banton. Sound recorders, Earl Hayman and Don Johnson. Running time, 95 minutes. Released March 12, 1937.

With Charlie Arnt and Fred MacMurray.

[143]

With Fred MacMurray.

CAST

Carole Lombard (*Maggie King*); Fred MacMurray (*Skid Johnson*); Charles Butterworth (*Harry*); Jean Dixon (*Ella*); Dorothy Lamour (*Anita Alvarez*); Harvey Stephens (*Harvey Dexter*); Cecil Cunningham (*Murphy*); Charlie Arnt (*Georgie*); Franklin Pangborn (*Henri*); Anthony Quinn (*The Don*); Bud Flanagan (*The purser*); Charles Judels (*Tony*).

SYNOPSIS

Sailing from New York, Maggie King, an entertainer, becomes acquainted with Skid Johnson, a trumpeter. When their ship docks in Panama, Skid goes to work as a musician in a cabaret. At the club a fight breaks out between the trumpeter and the ill-tempered Don. Arrested and jailed, Skid loses his job and Maggie misses her ship to California.

Her financial resources exhausted, Maggie moves in with Skid and his friend Harry. She gives the flat a good cleaning and gets Skid a job playing the cornet at Murphy's cafe. Successful at Murphy's, Skid and Maggie are married. It is not long, however, before the musician is offered an opportunity to play in New York. Against Maggie's wishes, Skid goes north with an attractive young singer, Anita Alvarez.

Skid is a success in New York. Maggie, however, believes that

Skid no longer loves her and sues for a divorce. When Skid learns that Maggie is preparing to marry Harvey Dexter, he begins to lose interest in his career. Harry and Ella, Skid's old friends, encourage him to audition for an important radio program. They know that if Skid fails, his career will be ruined. The musician's spirit is re-kindled, however, when Maggie appears at the audition. Skid wins the radio contract and is reunited with Maggie.

REVIEWS

Frank S. Nugent,
The New York Times, April 15, 1937:
"Carole Lombard and Fred MacCurray skip through the formular devices of *Swing High, Swing Low* . . . with their usual ease at the Paramount, raising a routine story to a routine-plus picture. . . . *Swing High, Swing Low*, like most Ferris wheels, doesn't go any-where—at least, nowhere that you have not been. Its players really are worthy of better treatment."

Variety, April 21, 1937:
"Camera and general technique click throughout, including some brief but punchy montage by Farciot Edouart, who has so skillfully blended his special camera effects—the champagne bubbles, etc.—that it's almost part of the plot. The increasing usages, of late, of

With Fred MacMurray.

*With Fred MacMurray and
Dorothy Lamour (upper right).*

With Fred MacMurray.

unobtrusive but well-fitting montage to interpret dramatic screen moods, incidentally points the way to a new and finer film art."

Otis Ferguson,
The New Republic, May 5, 1937:
"The faults are easy to catalogue; the virtues are those of a good film comedy and about as easy to describe as running water, having the same continuous flow and play of light and change without effort and joy to the senses. Not just dialogue; not just the people who put it over; not just the situations they are put in; not just the clear development and right focus of everything in the cameras. It is a little of each of these and a lot of something else, some sunny genius for the total effect."

Nothing Sacred

Selznick-International / 1937

Released through United Artists. Directed by William Wellman. Produced by David O. Selznick. Screenplay by Ben Hecht. Based on the story by William Street. Photographed by W. Howard Greene. Special photographic effects, Jack Cosgrove. Musical score by Oscar Levant. Novelty music by Raymond Scott. Film editor, James E. Newcom. Assistant director, Frederick A. Spencer. Art direction, Lyle Wheeler. Costumes by Travis Banton and Walter Plunkett. Color by Technicolor. Running time, 75 minutes. Released November 26, 1937.

With Charles Winninger and Fredric March.

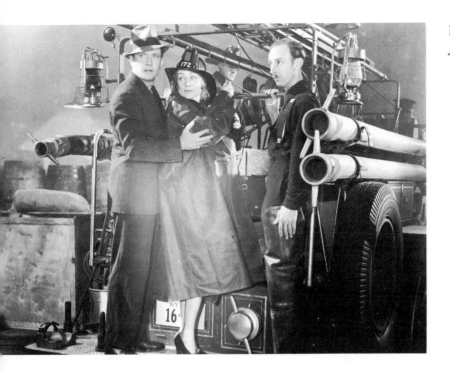

*With Fredric March and
John Qualen.*

With Fredric March.

CAST

Carole Lombard (*Hazel Flagg*); Fredric March (*Wally Cook*); Charles Winninger (*Dr. Downer*); Walter Connolly (*Stone*); Sig Berman (*Dr. Eggelhoffer*); Frank Fay (*Master of ceremonies*); Raymond Scott and his quintet (*Orchestra*); Maxie Rosenbloom (*Max*); Alex Schoenberg (*Dr. Kerchinwisser*); Monte Wooley (*Dr. Vunch*); (Alex Novinsky (*Dr. Marachuffsky*); Margaret Hamilton (*Drug store lady*); Troy Brown (*Ernest Walker*); Hattie McDaniels (*Mrs. Walker*); Katherine Shelton (*Dr. Donner's nurse*); Olin Howland (*Baggage man*); Ben Morgan (*Wrestler*); Hans Steinke (*Wrestler*); George Chandler (*Photographer*); Claire Du Brey (*Miss Rafferty*); Nora Cecil (*Schoolteacher*).

SYNOPSIS

Hazel Flagg, residing in Warsaw, Vermont, has always wanted to leave her village and visit New York City. One day Hazel is examined by the town physician, Dr. Downer, who tells her that she is the victim of radium poisoning and has only six months to live. Shortly afterward the doctor corrects his diagnosis and informs Hazel that she is well.

The story of her impending death, however, reaches New York City where it is exploited by Wally Cook of *The Morning Star.* Cook, at the moment out of favor with his publisher, Stone, sees in the case of the dying girl an opportunity to regain his position by increasing the circulation of the *Star.*

With Stone's concurrence, Cook arranges to bring the girl to

With Walter Connolly and Fredric March.

New York. Hazel persuades Downer to maintain the fiction of her impending death in order that she may realize her dream of visiting New York.

The *Star's* campaign is sensational. Following her arrival in Manhattan the "dying girl" is presented the key to the city. As millions read of her tragic case, Hazel becomes America's sweetheart. She is talked about everywhere; even a wrestling match at Madison Square Garden stops ten seconds to pay her tribute. When Stone and those who sponsored her finally learn that Hazel is not going to die, they fear that she will publicly reveal the truth. But Hazel, who has fallen in love with Cook, agrees to stage a "suicide" in order to save the reporter's reputation. While Cook and Hazel, disguised in sunglasses, secretly sail away, the Governor declares a holiday for her funeral.

With Fredric March.

With Margaret Hamilton, Fredric March, and Walter Connolly.

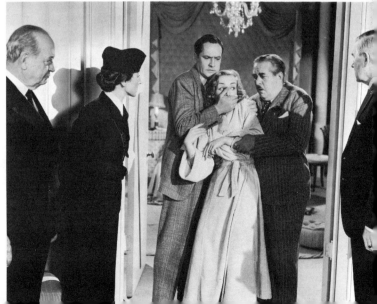

REVIEWS

Gus McCarthy,
Motion Picture Herald. August 21, 1937:
"Mr. Selznick will attempt to prove . . . that there's nothing sacred in the hypothesis that newspaper stories have been done to death."

William R. Weaner,
The Motion Picture Herald, November 27, 1937:
"Although an unusual offering from the studios of David O. Selznick, noted for turning out a more orthodox and simple type of entertainment in the grand manner, *Nothing Sacred* is as finely accoutered, technically, as his serious works."

Variety, December 1, 1937:
"*Nothing Sacred* sets a strong pace at the beginning, holding it steadily for most of the way, and then strikes a climax with the fight scene between Miss Lombard and Fredric March. That's the topper and one of the best laugh scenes ever put on the screen."

Time, December 6, 1937:
"*Nothing Sacred* is for the most part competently managed entertainment, but its trouble is that its characters have to behave to fit an artificial plot. March and Lombard, however, work hard to conceal this handicap and, good troupers that they are, seldom show the perspiration their effort requires."

Peter Galway,
The New Statesman and Nation, February 12, 1938:
"The direction of William Wellman translates Hecht's script into excellent cinema, and the acting is superb. . . ."

Basil Wright,
The Spectator (London), February 18, 1938:
"Because there is at the least a demi-cauldron of good honest hate about it, *Nothing Sacred* makes all the other crazy comedies look rather drab. It will be seen that it is hardly a plot for the squeamish or the shockable; there is only one person who has any sense of decency at all, and that is the reporter (Fredric March), whose married prospects with the unscrupulous minx one cannot help viewing with deep concern. There is indeed, a fundamental distaste for humanity here, which might have given the film something approaching the lusty hatred of a play like *Volpone;* but this the producers, quite rightly doubtful of the public stomach, have carefully avoided. The film remains funny, packed with incident and with exceedingly clever dialogue, and because it does at least hold up a mirror, even though it be a disturbing mirror, to a very real world of ballyhoo and cheap sensationalism the pleasure to be obtained from it is something more than the usual mulish guffaw."

With Fredric March.

True Confession

Paramount / 1937

Directed by Wesley Ruggles. Produced by Albert Lewin. Screenplay by Claude Binyon. Based on the play, *Mon Crime,* by Louis Verneuil and Georges Berr. Photographed by Ted Tetzlaff. Musical direction, Boris Morros. Original musical score by Frederick Hollander. Song: "True Confession," by Frederick Hollander and Sam Caslow. Film editor, Paul Weatherwax. Art direction, Hans Drier and Robert Usher. Interior decorations, A. E. Freudeman. Costumes by Travis Banton. Sound recorders, Earl Hàyman and Don Johnson. Running time, 84 minutes. Released December 24, 1937.

With John T. Murray.

With Una Merkel and director Wesley Ruggles.

[151]

With Edgar Kennedy.

CAST

Carole Lombard (*Helen Bartlett*); Fred MacMurray (*Kenneth Bartlett*); John Barrymore (*Charley*); Una Merkel (*Daisy McClure*); Porter Hall (*Prosecutor*); Edgar Kennedy (*Darsey*); Lynne Overman (*Bartender*); Fritz Field (*Krayler's butler*); Richard Carle (*Judge*); John T. Murray (*Otto Krayler*); Tommy Dugan (*Typewriter man*); Garry Owen (*Tony Krauch*); Toby Wing (*Suzanne Baggart*); Hattie McDaniel (*Ella*); Bernard Suss (*Pedestrian*).

With Fred MacMurray and Porter Hall.

SYNOPSIS

Helen Bartlett becomes the secretary to wealthy Otto Krayler in an effort to help her husband, Kenneth, an idealistic young attorney who refuses to take a case unless convinced of the innocence or honesty of his client. Her employment, however, is of short duration. When Krayler becomes too affectionate, Helen punches him and quits her job. Later, Krayler is mysteriously murdered and Helen is accused of the crime. Kenneth, refusing to believe that Helen is not responsible for Krayler's death, enters a plea of justifiable homicide in defense of chastity. After a highly publicized trial the jury returns a verdict of not guilty. The trial brings the attorney new clients, while Helen receives an offer to publish her life story.

One day Helen is approached by Charley, an eccentric derelict, who claims to know something about Krayler's death. He threatens to tell Kenneth the truth unless Helen agrees to pay him a sum of money. Overhearing Charley's threats, Kenneth enters the room. Charley confesses to the Bartlett's that his brother-in-law, who has since died in an auto crash, murdered Krayler. Charley then departs, realizing there is no hope of collecting blackmail.

Having learned the truth at last, Kenneth prepares to leave his wife. To prevent his departure, Helen tells Kenneth that he is going to be a father. He soon discovers that she has told another lie. Realizing, however, that he cannot live without her, Kenneth lifts Helen into his arms and carries her into the house.

With Fred MacMurray.

REVIEWS

James Francis Crow,
The Hollywood Citizen News, November 17, 1937:
"Miss Lombard plunges headlong into her role, and comes through

With Una Merkel.

*With Fred MacMurray and
John Barrymore.*

with a vigorous piece of trouping which will delight her fans, and
win her many new ones."

Frank Nugent,
The New York Times, December 16, 1937:
"But over them all is Miss Lombard, a tower of comic strength,
and the pivotal point around which the picture spins."

London Times, December 20, 1937:
"The trial, with the husband superbly emotional, is a hilarious
satire on certain aspects of the American judicial system, and lifts
it far above the general run of film comedies. Miss Lombard is
delightful—her complete belief in the emotional portrait, as drawn

On the set with Fred MacMurray.

*With Una Merkel and
John Barrymore.*

With Fred MacMurray, Tom Duggan and Una Merkel.

by her husband, of her feelings at the time of a murder she did not commit is a real joy."

Basil Wright,
The Spectator (London), December 31, 1937:
"*True Confession*, you will by now have gathered, is a carefully calculated essay in controlled lunacy—controlled, because it is nearly always true enough to the humanities to remain curiously convincing, lunatic chiefly because of John Barrymore's macabre performance as the blackmailing criminologist, whose screw is well and truly turned, and who veers in a nightmare-ish manner from slapstick to something bordering on the 'cauld grue.' The rest of the cast, notably Edgar Kennedy as a pent-up detective, Fred MacMurray as the amiable victim of connubiality, and Porter Hall as a Groucho-like prosecutor, festoon themselves gracefully round the tower of lies which Miss Lombard, *splendide mendax* and charming to the last, erects and demolishes at her own sweet will. British studios might also note the interesting fact that, apart from the players' salaries, the production costs of this film must have been quite small. There is one large set—the court scene; but the rest of the action takes place in small and economical domestic interiors or in the open air. So much the better."

With Fred MacMurray.

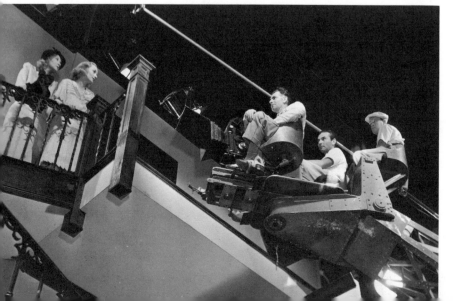

With Una Merkel, director Wesley Ruggles and cinematographer Ted Tetzlaff.

[155]

With Fernand Gravet.

Fools for Scandal

Warner Bros. / 1938

Directed and produced by Mervyn Le Roy. Screenplay by Herbert and Joseph Fields. Additional dialogue by Irving Beecher. Based on the play, *Return Engagement,* by Nancy Hamilton, James Shute and Rosemary Casey. Photographed by Ted Tetzlaff. Music director, Leo F. Forbstein. Music and lyrics by Richard Rogers and Lorens Hart. Orchestral arrangements by Adolph Deutsch. "Le Petite Harlem" sequence directed by Bobby Connolly. Film editor, William Holmes. Art direction, Anton Grot. Gowns by Milo Anderson. Miss Lombard's gowns by Travis Banton. Sound recorders, E. A. Brown and David Forrest. Running time, 81 minutes. Released April 16, 1938.

CAST

Carole Lombard (*Kay Winters*); Fernand Gravet (*Réné*); Ralph Bellamy (*Phillip Chester*); Allen Jenkins (*Dewey Gibson*); Isabel Jeans (*Lady Paula Malveston*); Marie Wilson (*Myrtle*); Marcia Ralston (*Jill*); Tola Nesmith (*Agnes*); Heather Thatcher (*Lady Potter-Porter*); Jacques Lory (*Papa*); Tempe Piggott (*Bessie*); Michellette Burani (*Mme. Brioche*); Teni LeGon (*Specialty*).

SYNOPSIS

One afternoon while strolling in the vicinity of Montmartre, Réné, an impoverished young nobleman, encounters Kay Winters, a famous American film star. Having no knowledge of one another's real identity, they exchange pleasantries, ride about town in a taxi, and dine later at a fashionable cafe.

After Kay's return to London, Réné appears without invitation at her Noah's Ark party. Kay jokingly offers him employment in her home as a servant. Réné, who very much wants to be near her, accepts a position as cook and butler.

In a most amusing manner the butler succeeds in preventing Phillip Chesterton from proposing to Kay. The love affair between the nobleman and the film star is sealed when they stroll out into the fog and embrace in a mysterious dark building. Suddenly the lights go up and they are seen standing on the stage of a theatre in the midst of a performance.

REVIEWS

Variety, March 15, 1938:
"For a picture of its pretentions and talented personnel, this falls short of distinction and is in many respects pretty dull stuff. It is Carole Lombard's first film for Warners and Fernand Gravet's second in America. For Gravet it is not necessarily an accurate gauge as to his ultimate reception by the American public; for Carole Lombard it must be reckoned below her usual standard, and for the director-producer it is not up to the Mervyn LeRoy par."

Time, April 4, 1938:
"In spite of Carole Lombard's strident earthiness, the result is as unearthly as Actor Gravet's French-flavored concave British inflection, as wooden as Charlie McCarthy—whom Actor Gravet, in claw-hammer coat and starchy shirt front, resembles more that he does [Edward] Windsor."

Photoplay, June, 1938:
"It's not a good metaphor to call several reels of film a straw but anyway this is the one that probably will break the back of that slapstick camel Carole Lombard's been riding so long . . . inane, pointless . . . warmed-over film material."

With Fernand Gravet.

With Ralph Bellamy and Fernand Gravet.

[157]

With James Stewart.

Made for Each Other

Selznick-International / 1939

Released through United Artists. Directed by John Cromwell. Produced by David O. Selznick. Production designed by William Cameron Menzies. Photographed by Leon Shamroy. Special photographic effects by Jack Cosgrove. Music by Lou Forbes. Film editor, James E. Newcom. Assistant director, Eric Stacey. Art direction, Lyle Wheeler. Interior decorations, Edward G. Boyle. Costumes by Travis Banton. Sound recorder, Jack Noyes. Con-

With director John Cromwell and producer David O. Selznick.

tributor to the humorous situations, Frank Ryan. Research, Lilian K. Dighton. Running time, 90 minutes. Released February 10, 1939.

CAST

Carole Lombard (*Jane Mason*); James Stewart (*John Mason*); Charles Coburn (*Judge Doolittle*); Lucile Watson (*Mrs. Mason*); Eddie Quillar (*Conway*); Alma Kruger (*Sister Madeline*); Ruth Weston (*Eunice Doolittle*); Donald Briggs (*Carter*); Harry Davenport (*Dr. Healy*); Esther Dale (*First cook*); Renee Orsell (*Second cook*); Louise Beavers (*Third cook*); Ward Bond (*Hatton*); Olin Howland (*Farmer*); Ferm Emmett (*Farmer's wife*); Bonnie Belle Barber (*John Mason, Jr.* [*newly born*]); Jackie Taylor (*John Mason, Jr.* [*one year old*]); Mickey Rentschler (*Office boy*); Ivan Simpson (*Simon*).

SYNOPSIS

Attorney John Mason and his wife, Jane, have boarded a transatlantic liner for a honeymoon cruise to Europe. The trip is cancelled, however, when Mason's boss, Judge Doolittle, orders that he return to try an important case. It is the first of a series of disappointments which the newlyweds experience.

Jane and John Mason entertain the Judge, his daughter Eunice and her husband Carter at a humorously tragic dinner party. As the last course is served, melted ice cream, Doolittle announces that his son-in-law, Carter, has been made a partner in the firm.

Life grows more difficult for the Masons. Unpaid bills accumulate, Mason's fault-finding mother comes to live in their small apartment, and on New Year's eve their baby suffers a serious illness.

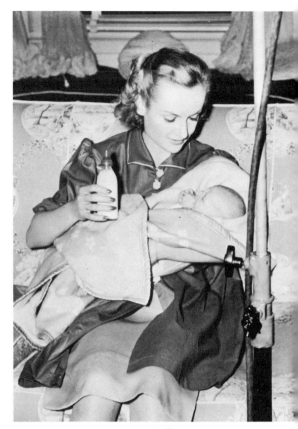

A rehearsal with Bonnie Belle Barber, ten days old.

With James Stewart.

With Charles Coburn, Esther Dale, and Donald Briggs.

Only when the Mason baby is dying does Judge Doolittle seem to recognize the worth of the young attorney. Doolittle makes it possible for the baby's medicine to be flown through a blinding snowstorm to New York. The infant's life is saved and Mason achieves success, becoming a partner in the firm.

REVIEWS

Newsweek, February 13, 1939:

"It is several years since Carole Lombard has been able to quiet down to a straight dramatic role. With David O. Selznick's *Made for Each Other,* the flighty blonde of screwball-comedy fame gets the chance and makes the most of it. In giving what is probably the best performance of her career, she shares the film's honors with its author, director, and her co-star, James Stewart.

Philip T. Hastung,

Commonweal, February 24, 1939:

"The cinder in Jane's eye, which led to his meeting and marrying Jane, is what Johnny falteringly talks about to his boss and later to his mother. Then there follows in *Made for Each Other,* a succession of homely scenes, expertly directed by John Cromwell, and sincerely and simply acted, that are real and pathetically touching as Johnny and Jane are taught that marriage is a serious business, a partnership. The young couple could be any young couple during the first years of marriage. There are a few exaggerations: perhaps the apartment is too expensive-looking, or Johnny is too shy and stumbling in speech to be a lawyer, or the flyer's hazardous trip

With Harry Davenport.

With Lucile Watson.

With Harry Davenport and James Stewart.

with the serum for the dying child is too melodramatic. Forget those faults and concentrate on Johnny when he is crushed because he thinks he's a failure, or on Jane when she is led by the nun to pray for the baby. I'll guarantee you'll want to stand up and applaud for this Selznick production of Jo Swerling's screenplay, for James Stewart who makes you perspire when he asks the boss for a raise, for Lucile Watson who plays the part of Johnny's mother with keen understanding, and for the new and different Carole Lombard who has stopped being a screwball comedienne and is convincing as the young wife."

Time, February 27, 1939:

"*Made for Each Other* was produced by David Oliver Selznick, directed by John Cromwell, written by Jo Swerling and acted, principally, by James Stewart and Carole Lombard. Which of these deserves most credit for the indisputable fact that this mundane, domestic chronicle has more dramatic impact than all the hurricanes, sandstorms and earthquakes manufactured in Hollywood last season is a mystery which does not demand solution. What does demand solution is why, when Hollywood can make pictures as sound as *Made for Each Other,* it practically never does."

*With Jackie Taylor and
James Stewart.*

With Nella Walker.

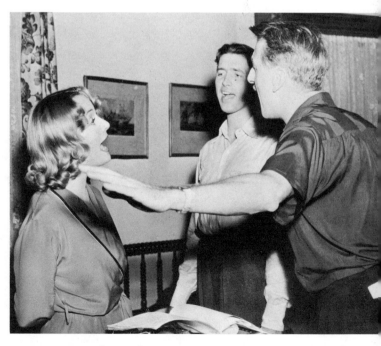

*With James Stewart and director
John Cromwell.*

In Name Only

RKO Radio / 1939

Directed by John Cromwell. Produced by George Haight. Pandro S. Berman in charge of production. Screenplay by Richard Sherman. Based on the novel, *Memory of Love*, by Bessie Brewer. Photographed by J. Roy Hunt. Music by Roy Webb. Film editor, William Hamilton. Assistant director, Dewey Starkey. Art direction, Van Nest Polglase. Associate art director, Perry Ferguson. Set decoration, Darrell Silvera. Gowns by Edward Stevenson. Miss Lombard's gowns by Irene. Sound recorder, Hugh McDowell, Jr. Running time, 92 minutes. Released August 18, 1939.

CAST

Carole Lombard (*Julie Eden*); Cary Grant (*Alec Walker*); Kay Francis (*Maida Walker*); Charles Coburn (*Mr. Walker*); Helen Vinson (*Suzanne*); Katharine Alexander (*Laura*); Jonathan Hale (*Dr. Gateson*); Maurice Moscovitch (*Dr. Muller*); Nella Walker (*Mrs. Walker*); Peggy Ann Gardner (*Ellen*); Spencer Charters (*Gardner*).

SYNOPSIS

Julie Eden, a young widow, rents a summer cottage in Connecticut near the estate of Alec Walker. Having fallen in love with Julie,

With Cary Grant.

With Cary Grant.

Alec seeks a divorce from his wife Maida, a woman who married him for position and money. The scheming Maida appears to give in, promising Alec that she will obtain a divorce in Paris. But upon her return to New York, Maida tells Alec that she never intended to divorce him. In a venomous tone, she threatens to sue Julie for alienation of affection should Alec sue for divorce. Julie and Alec leave Maida's suite convinced that they have little chance for happiness. Later that night, Alec develops a serious case of pneumonia. Outside the hospital sickroom, Maida tells Julie that she is only interested in Alec's money and the fortune that his father will leave someday. Having overheard Maida's remarks, Alec's parents understand her true character for the first time. It is understood that it will now be possible for Julie and Alec to marry.

With Jonathan Hale, Cary Grant, and Kay Francis.

[163]

With Kay Francis.

REVIEWS

Bosley Crowther,
The New York Times, August 4, 1939:
"Miss Lombard plays her poignant role with all the fragile intensity and contained passion that have lifted her to dramatic eminince."

Graham Greene,
The Spectator (London), December 8, 1939:
"This is a well-made little picture of unhappy marriage. It is often sentimental, but the general impression which remains is quite an authentic one—a glossy photographic likeness of gloom: fruitless discussions about Reno, polite chicanery over the long-distance phone, hate in the sherry glass, the rattled nerve and the despair of any day being different from today. *Dodsworth* and *Craig's Wife* come to mind: those, too, were pictures of mental distress among the higher incomes, but *Dodsworth,* at any rate, had more saving humor. Humor here pops up only incidentally—with a drunk little clerk on Christmas Eve (surprisingly acted by that icy gangster, Mr. Allen Baxter), with a scared fat youth in a restaurant-car listening to the forked war of women's tongues. I wonder sometimes where pictures like this find the money for production: the huge cinema masses surely have a shorter and sharper way of satisfying their loves and hates: are they not a little puzzled and bored by the well-groomed classy tragedy with a happy ending, the sense of sex isolated from any other kind of trouble, money or work, what Mr. Aiken has described so well as 'the late night wrangles, the three-day silences, the weepings in dark rooms face downward on dishevelled beds . . . the livid eyes of hate over the morning grapefruit?'

"The picture is made, quite creditably, by three people—Miss Carole Lombard, Mr. Cary Grant and Miss Kay Francis. Both actresses break new ground. Miss Lombard's wavering and melancholy voice, her bewildered eyes, which have in the past faltered so well among the rapid confused events of crazy comedy, work just as satisfactorily here—wringing out tears instead of laughs, and Miss Francis, 'the best-dressed woman in Hollywood,' who used to step unresiliently, with a lisp, through glamorous parts, for the first time grips our attention as the hard unscrupulous wife who is after something more valuable than alimony, her father-in-law's money. I liked this wholeheartedly unpleasant character, who presents a cunning picture of understanding and patience to the parents, driving a wedge between them and their son, and when at last her husband's open preference for another woman forces her consent to a divorce, double-crosses relentlessly—going to Paris with the parents on the secret understanding that there she will break the truth to them and get her decree, but all the time determined to hold on, inventing delay after delay to sap the girl's trust in her lover, until she at last returns without it. The main theme of the picture is the strain of waiting on the Paris line and listening to the time-saving lies: the

With Kay Francis.

atmosphere of triumphant war between a woman with complete mastery of her feelings and her tongue and an ordinary kindly man and a rather guileless girl.

"But this is a classy, not a first-class picture. Shot with a refined taste for interior decoration, well-groomed, advertising only the best cars, it is oversweetened with the material for tears: Miss Lombard's young widow has a small child addicted to winsome wisecracks; the last hope of divorce crashes on Christmas Eve, with the parcels stacked beside the tree and the candles ready for lighting; the hero lies traditionally drunk before the open window of a seedy hotel. Here the film comes to life again for a few minutes with the fine study of the hotel manager—the narrow prudish face, the sly suggestion, the cigarette-case always open in the palm, the sacred secretive lechery. But after that brief appearance the well-worn path of the tear-jerker has to be trodden to the bitter and the happy end. Pneumonia, the girl forbidden the bedside, the old specialist saying, 'There is only one person who can give him the will to live,' the white lie—'everything is all right now,' and then the wife's arrival, the rash betrayal of what she's really after while the parents listen out of sight, everything cleared satisfactorily up in a few seconds, even the pneumonia—'he's sleeping now,' just as though the slow dubious movements of the human intelligence could be shot by an ultra-rapid camera, happiness seeded and budded and blossomed with the knowing speed of a *Secrets of Nature* flower."

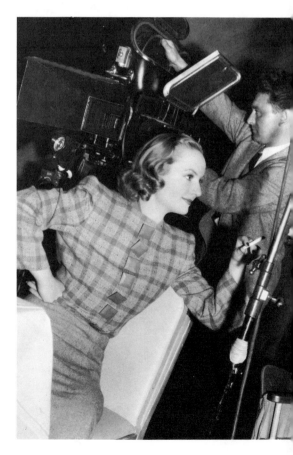

Vigil in the Night

RKO Radio / 1940

Directed and produced by George Stevens. Pandro S. Berman in charge of production. Screenplay by Fred Guidl, P. J. Wolfson, Rowland Leigh. Based on the novel by A. J. Cronin. Photographed by Robert de Grasse. Music by Alfred Newman. Film editor, Henry Berman. Assistant director, Syd Fogel. Art direction, Van Nest Polglase. Associate art director, L. P. Williams. Set decorations, Darrell Silvera. Costumes by Walter Plunkett. Running time, 94 minutes. Released February 9, 1940.

CAST

Carole Lombard (*Anne Lee*); Brian Aherne (*Dr. Prescott*); Anne Shirley (*Lucy Lee*); Julien Mitchell (*Matthew Bowley*); Robert

Coote (*Dr. Caley*); Brenda Forbes (*Nora*); Rita Page (*Glennie*); Peter Cushing (*Joe Shand*); Ethel Griffies (*Matron East*) Doris Lloyd (*Mrs. Bowley*); Emily Fitzroy (*Sister Gilson*).

SYNOPSIS

In Manchester, England, Anne Lee, a dedicated nurse, assumes the guilt for the death of a child which resulted from the negligence of her younger sister, nurse Lucy Lee. Remaining faithful to her profession, Anne goes to another hospital where she meets and falls in love with Dr. Prescott who is seeking financial support for a new addition to the hospital. A scandal results in Anne's dismissal, but when an epidemic strikes she returns to the hospital to give service. Her sister dies during the epidemic, while Anne, who has shown unselfish devotion to duty, is restored to her position and reunited with Prescott. All ends happily when the trustees award Prescott the new hospital facility.

REVIEWS

Motion Picture Herald, February 10, 1940:
"[*Vigil in the Night*] is a scorching protest, uttered in the dramatic form, grim from start to finish and often violently realistic. It makes its point powerfully.... *Vigil in the Night* is splendidly produced and inescapably effective as a document. It is not in any way a

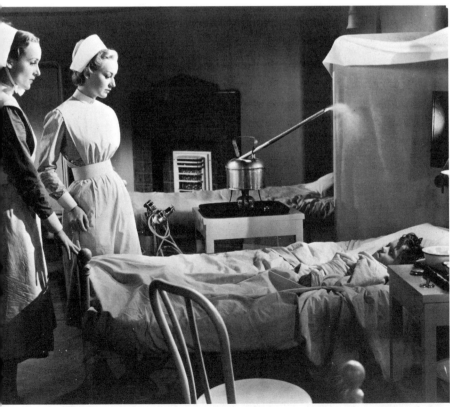

With Anne Shirley.

With Brian Aherne.

pleasant picture, nor is it intended to be. Carole Lombard gives a commanding portrayal of the austerely fervent nurse who shelters her sister and struggles on to exemplify the ideals of her profession."

Time, March 11, 1940:
"*Vigil in the Night* never quite develops enough inner drama to lighten its encircling gloom."

London Times, May 27, 1940:
"*Vigil in the Night* has been made with a painstaking sincerity, and both acting and directing are level-headed and restrained, but inspiration is lacking and the film never touches the heights."

With Brian Aherne.

With Charles Laughton.

They Knew What They Wanted

RKO Radio / 1940

Directed by Garson Kanin. Produced by Erich Pommer. Executive producer, Harry E. Edington. Screenplay by Robert Ardrey. Based on the play, *They Knew What They Wanted*, by Sidney Howard. Photographed by Harry Stradling. Special effects, Vernon L. Walker. Music by Alfred Newman. Film editor, John Sturges. Assistant director, Ruby Rosenberg. Art direction, Van Nest Polglase. Associate art director, Mark-Lee Kirk. Set decorations, Darrell Silvera. Costumes by Edward Stevenson. Sound recorder, John L. Cass. Running time. 90 minutes. Released October 25, 1940.

CAST

Carole Lombard (*Amy Peters*); Charles Laughton (*Tony Patucci*); William Gargan (*Joe*); Harry Carey (*The doctor*); Frank Fay (*Father McKee*); Joe Bernard (*The R.F.D.*); Janet Fox (*Mildred*); Lee Tung-Foo (*Ah Gee*); Karl Malden (*Red*); Victor Kilian (*The photographer*); Paul Lepers (*Hired hand*).

SYNOPSIS

Amy, a waitress in San Francisco, agrees to marry Tony Patucci, a man she has never seen. The shy and unattractive Tony, a rancher in the Napa Valley, seals the marriage proposal by enclosing a photo of Joe, his handsome hired man. Only after her arrival at the ranch does Amy discover Tony's real identity.

On the night before his wedding, Tony has an accident at the fiesta, breaking both legs. Amy resents Tony at first, turning her affection to Joe. Cynical about love, the hired man indicates that he is not interested in marriage because he does not "owe no man nothing—or no woman." Amy, however, wants a home and if "her husband wants kids, that's okay."

While Tony recuperates, the woman he cherishes becomes pregnant with Joe's child. After a fight with Joe, Tony forgives Amy who goes away to have her baby. It is understood that she, having recognized her mistake, will return to Tony and happiness.

REVIEWS

Basil Wright,
The Spectator (London), January 10, 1941:
"The story has been well adapted for the screen by Robert Ardrey (author of *Thunder Rock*), and is beautifully directed by Garson Kanin under Erich Pommer's producership. Kanin is a sentimentalist, but he also commands a realism which is based on observation and understanding of ordinary people. Note the scene at the fiesta, when the crowd of Italian guests, hushed suddenly, moves from window to window outside the lighted house as Tony is carried to his room. Every person, every gesture, is easy, natural, spontaneous, and, in a phrase, absolutely true to life. This sequence, by the way, is one of the many pieces of really first-class camerawork by Harry Stradling with which the film is graced. Carole Lombard, under Kanin, proves a much more talented actress than one had supposed; both she and William Gargan, as the assistant, stand up splendidly to Laughton's moving sincerity no less than to his enormous acting technique. But it is curious that Frank Fay—Hollywood's foremost satirical actor—should have been miscast as a prosy padre whose intrusions into the story are intolerably well meant. And finally the eruption of a lush musical score at all the dramatic points is merely an insult to the vocal orchestration of the cast."

Otis Ferguson,
The New Republic, October 21, 1940:
"There are some fine things in the last part, words said and actions taken, the sentimental and the gay too; Laughton is fine as the Italo-American, almost letter-perfect and very jocund; Miss Lombard is at her best; and Harry Carey is as wonderful and right as ever—he is cast as the country doctor and damned if I wouldn't let him operate right now, though as he says, 'Lady, the things I don't know you could herd like cows.' Everyone does the best with what

he's got, and there is no truth lost by the way—in fact there is some truth achieved in it that we don't often get. But there is that story uncertainty and that forced ending; and so you have to admit that it wobbles on its pins occasionally at the same time you say that for dialogue, acting, background and film creation it's a honey."

Philip T. Hartung,
Commonweal, October 25, 1940:
"In this Erich Pommer production, Robert Ardrey's script has changed the Howard play, but has retained the spirit of the original drama, and Garson Kanin's intelligent direction has resulted in a poignant, sincere, adult film about three people who seem pathetically dumb and helpless but who are real people who know what they want."

Theatre Arts, December, 1940:
"Garson Kanin, who directed *They Knew What They Wanted* for RKO is, compared to Chaplin and Ford, a newcomer to the movies. A recent product of George Abbott's unofficial 'School of Dramatic Art' on Broadway, he moved on to Hollywood about three years ago and immediately made his mark as one of filmdom's young hopefuls. In *They Knew What They Wanted,* he again shows himself to be a resourceful director with a sharp sense of the dramatic, who can handle his actors with authority.

"Sidney Howard's play about Tony, the aging Italian grape grower, who wins himself a beautiful young wife by correspondence, has been filmed twice before, but with little success, since the industry's own censors both times cut into it so deep as to destroy it In this third film version there are again mysterious changes which can only be accounted for by censorship or fear of it. The Padre has turned so sweet as to be maudlin at times; the tough, practical nature of the stage Amy has been toned down; and her baby becomes the product of seduction rather than adultery, which casts a peculiar light on Hollywood's code of morals. Yet, except for a certain aura of softness about the picture, the wholehearted earthy spirit of the original play is there, thanks chiefly to Kanin, and to the script prepared by Robert Ardrey.

"Charles Laughton establishes Tony with a sure touch on the Italian's first entrance, fat and resplendent in his Sunday suit, with a handsome black hat on his head and, in his hand, patent leather shoes 'for da feet.' 'Looka me! I'm da most stylish fella in da world,' he roars, and vain and simple Tony, the man of hearty emotions, stands revealed. Laughton seldom falters in his characterization, which is the more remarkable because the ingenuous Tony is far from his usual field of endeavor. Carole Lombard, as Amy the wife who was wooed at long distance, has also moved afield for the part, but she too carries it with assurance. William Gargan's Joe, the migratory worker who leads Amy astray, suffers from the distortion of his part by the censor's evident insistence that he be a deep-dyed villain.

With William Gargan.

With Charles Laughton.

[171]

"When the director was allowed to make his own revisions on the stage version the results were more fortunate. The high point of the film is the fiesta before Tony and Amy get married, which was heard offstage in the play. It is a festival of wine, with dancing and gay songs, daring stunts and a rousing climax when Tony shows off for Amy's benefit once too often, and falls off the roof of his house. Garson Kanin's crowds in this scene move fluidly, and their sudden collapse from the roisterous fiesta mob to the sober and frightened little groups that gather about the house after Tony's fall heightens a dramatic moment.

"Kanin does not yet take full advantage of one of the greatest resources available to him, the camera. The picture is sometimes still, a little like a photographic record of a play, because the camera is so often stationary, like the eye of a theatre audience. The value of the camera is its flexibility, its power to search out all the angles of a situation for a rounded picture, or to pick out one angle and give it point. Because it can so often say things that words cannot, the camera is an instrument well worth mastering as this talented director has already mastered his other movie resources."

*With Harry Carey, Frank Fay,
and Charles Laughton.*

Mr. and Mrs. Smith

RKO Radio / 1941

Directed by Alfred Hitchcock. Executive producer, Harry E. Edington. Story and screenplay by Norman Krasna. Photographed by Harry Stradling. Special photographic effects, Vernon L. Walker. Music by Edward Ward. Film editor, William Hamilton. Art direction, Van Nest Polglase. Running time, 90 minutes. Released January 31, 1941.

CAST

Carole Lombard (*Ann Smith*); Robert Montgomery (*David Smith*); Gene Raymond (*Jeff Custer*); Jack Carson (*Chuck Benson*); Philip Merivale (*Mr. Custer*); Lucile Watson (*Mrs. Custer*); William Tracy (*Sammy*); Charles Halton (*Mr. Deever*); Esther

With Robert Montgomery.

Dale (*Mrs. Krausheimer*); Emma Dunn (*Martha*); William Edmunds (*Proprietor Lucy's*); Betty Compson (*Gertie*); Patricia Farr (*Gloria*); Adele Pearce (*Lily*).

SYNOPSIS

David and Ann Smith, a young Manhattan couple, have pledged never to leave one another in the midst of a quarrel. A disagreement on one occasion required the Smiths to remain together for eight days. In their most recent quarrel the argumentative Smiths have been confined to their bedroom for three days. When the quarrel is settled, Ann asks her husband at breakfast, "Darling, if you had to do it all over, would you marry me?" Mr. Smith, who

With Georgia Carroll, James Flavin and Gene Raymond.

[174]

With Gene Raymond.

really loves his wife, replies in a teasing manner, "Honestly, no."

At the office that morning, Mr. Smith is visited by a man who explains that because of a technicality the Smiths are not legally married. When David returns home that evening he does not realize that the man also visited Mrs. Smith. Remembering her husband's comment at breakfast, Ann is hopeful that her husband will suggest that they get married immediately.

That evening the Smiths make a valiant attempt to relive their courtship. They dine at an Italian restaurant, fondly remembered, but which has now changed hands. After a disastrous dinner the

With Gene Raymond.

With Gene Raymond.

Smiths return home. Convinced that David has no intention of legalizing their marriage, Ann locks Mr. Smith out of the bedroom and assumes her maiden name. David, meanwhile, takes up residence at his club.

Jeff Custer, Smith's legal partner, hopes to marry Ann now that the Smiths have separated. David, however, is determined to win her back. He follows Ann and Custer to a winter resort at Lake Placid. Satisfied that David loves her, Ann agrees to a reconciliation.

With Robert Montgomery and Gene Raymond.

With Robert Montgomery.

REVIEWS

Hollywood Reporter, January 16, 1941:
"It may be disappointing to many of the followers of Norman Krasna, Alfred Hitchcock and Carole Lombard who expected extreme brilliance from the trio, but there's enough fun in it to send you home happy with your entertainment."

Otis Ferguson,
The New Republic, March 4, 1941:
"When comedy was incidental to his story, Hitchcock did well enough with it always; but this time he goes heavy on us, he tries very hard and throws things about."

Louis MacNeice,
The Spectator (London), April 4, 1941:
"Mr. Montgomery and Miss Carole Lombard . . . have shown themselves adept in this genre, but this time the action drags; I found myself thinking nostalgically of *My Man Godfrey,* where Miss Lombard, playing opposite Mr. William Powell, got pretty near the zenith of her zany sex-appeal and highball farce, compared with which her latest performance is flat. . . . Perhaps we are getting a little tired of these high-life marital whimsies, where the husbands and wives have infinite leisure to throw tantrums and bottles, and such, and be reconciled and start all over with lots of new dishes to break."

[177]

Rehearsing To Be or Not to Be *with Ernst Lubitsch and Jack Benny. Lubitsch gave Lombard "a new quality," wrote Edgar Anstey, "some of the ignis fatuus of Garbo, some languors from Dietrich, but beneath the new things her own personal freshness and warmth."*

To Be or Not to Be

United Artists / 1942

Directed and produced by Ernst Lubitsch. Presented by Alexander Korda. Screenplay by Edwin Justus Mayer. From the story by Ernst Lubitsch and Melchior Lengyel. Photographed by Rudolph Mate. Special photographic effects by Lawrence Butler. Music by Werner Heyman. Film editor, Dorothy Spencer. Production design, and art direction, Vincent Korda. Makeup artist, Gordon Bau. Running time, 99 minutes. Released February 15, 1942.

CAST

Carole Lombard (*Maria Tura*); Jack Benny (*Joseph Tura*); Robert Stack (*Lieutenant Stanislav Sobinski*); Felix Bressart (*Greenberg*); Lionel Atwill (*Rawitch*); Stanley Ridges (*Professor Siletsky*); Sir Ruman (*Colonel Ehrhardt*); Tom Duggan (*Bronski*); Charles Halton (*Dobosh*); Henry Victor (*Captain Schulz*); Maude Eburne (*Anna*).

SYNOPSIS

A Polish theatrical company in Warsaw prepares to stage an anti-Nazi melodrama on the eve of the Second World War. Maria and Joseph Tura, whose specialty is Shakespeare, rehearse for the leading roles. The Polish government cancels the production, fearful that relations between Berlin and Warsaw will be worsened by the performance of a play critical of the Nazi regime. The players, somewhat disappointed, present *Hamlet* instead, with Maria and Joseph in the title roles.

When Tura begins Hamlet's soliloquy, "To be or not to be ...," Lieutenant Sobinski, a pilot in the Polish Air Force, visits Maria backstage. These meetings terminate, however, following the outbreak of war. With the collapse of Poland and its occupation by German forces, Sobinski flees to London while the Turas remain in Warsaw.

In London, Professor Siletsky, a Nazi agent posing as a Polish patriot, tells Sobinski and a group of Polish freedom fighters serving in the British Air Force, that he is returning to Warsaw on a secret

Tom Duggan as Hitler in the opening scene of To Be or Not to Be.

Jack Benny (on stage) and Robert Stack.

mission. Gaining the confidence of the Polish aviators, the professor secures the names and addresses of their friends and relatives in Warsaw. Lieutenant Sobinski innocently gives Siletsky the name of Maria Tura, "Poland's leading actress," but a figure unknown to the professor. Suspicious of Siletsky, Sobinski makes a report to British military intelligence. Convinced that Siletsky is an enemy, the British dispatch Sobinski to Warsaw with instructions to recover the list of names and addresses.

Upon his arrival in Warsaw, Sobinski is aided in the accomplishment of his mission by Maria Tura and the troupe of actors. Siletsky, meanwhile, has ordered Maria's arrest. Under escort, she is brought to the Gestapo agent's suite at the Hotel Europejski. After a short interview, Siletsky is satisfied that he has charmed Maria into joining the New Order. Siletsky is called away to confer with the Gestapo chief, Colonel Ehrhardt. The actors, masquerading as Nazi soldiers, take the professor to the theatre where he is presented to Joseph Tura, disguised as Ehrhardt. After learning the location of the list of names, Tura artificially extends the interview ("So they call me 'Concentration Camp Ehrhardt' "). Siletsky grows suspicious when Tura begins to ask questions about Maria's affair with Sobinski. Pointing his gun at the jealous husband, the Nazi agent escapes into the auditorium. Siletsky is shot a few moments later and dies on the stage where the actors had intended to present their anti-Nazi play.

In order to rescue Maria and secure the list of names, Tura returns to the hotel disguised as Siletsky. Later, Tura is arrested in Siletsky's disguise and brought to the office of the real Colonel Ehrhardt. As Ehrhardt prepares to unmask Tura, the actors, again

On the set with Robert Stack.

wearing Nazi uniforms, burst into the Gestapo chief's office and take Tura into "custody."

Having secured the list, the entire acting company, including Lieutenant Sobinski, masquerade as high ranking Nazis in order to make their escape from Warsaw. With Bronski impersonating Hitler, the actors appear at a theatre where the Führer is expected. Stealing his automobile, they drive to the airport and escape by plane. When the aircraft is safely over the British Isles, Bronski, still in disguise, orders the two German pilots to jump without parachutes. They obediently reply, "Ja, mein Führer," and exit from the plane.

With Jack Benny, Charles Halton, and Maude Eburne.

With Robert Stack and Jack Benny.

With Stanley Ridges.

The theatrical troupe parachutes to safety, landing on the property of a Scottish farmer. Catching sight of Bronski in the Hitler disguise, the farmer can only exclaim, "Oh, not him too!" The story ends in London, with Tura on stage as Hamlet. As he starts to deliver the famous soliloquy, a young naval officer in the front row rises to leave.

REVIEWS

Thornton Delehanty,
The New York Herald Tribune, November 30, 1941:
"It's the horror of war as seen through the eyes of a company of actors. The picture gives it a certain real-unreality which is meant to be comic, but not really broad comedy."

Variety, February 18, 1942:
"Carole Lombard's last picture needs no benefit of tragic circumstances to set it up as a strong money offering and to leave its impress of fine screen artistry. It is characteristic of the roles which were most becoming to Miss Lombard, lively with laughter, lush with entertainment, appropriate as the valedictory of a persuasive actress and a glowing personality."

The Film Daily, February 19, 1942:
"While the film is billed as a comedy, the fun is often rimmed with drama. It is reminiscent of a person trying to play the clown in a spirit of seriousness."

Film Music Notes, March, 1942:
"... the film is for the most part both entertaining and interesting and certainly never did Miss Lombard look lovelier nor act better.

It can be truly said that it will be a fitting picture by which to remember her. . . . Suspense is maintained throughout with just enough comedy and pathos blended for proper balance and perfect timing. The music is very well orchestrated and nicely adapted to emphasize national characteristics and the use of Chopin's Military Polonaise add special color both at the opening and at the close."

Life, March 9, 1942:
"In years to come the fact that Hollywood could convert part of a world crisis into such a cops and robbers charade will certainly be regarded as a remarkable phenomena."

Philip T. Hartung,
Commonweal, March 13, 1942:
"In directing this film, Ernst Lubitsch wasn't always too sure of himself; farce crosses pathos at times and runs toward madness. The production, however, is excellent; and the actors never let him

With Jack Benny.

down.... Many of the scenes are beautifully photographed. The suspense mounts to an exciting climax. The comedy is hilarious— even when it is hysterically thrilling."

Time, March 16, 1942:
"In *Ninotchka,* Director Ernst Lubitsch deliciously kidded the vagaries of the Soviets; in *To Be* he succeeds—as Hollywood had not yet done—in deftly ridiculing Hitler and the Nazis."

Manny Farber,
The New Republic, March 23, 1942:
"There is a lot of maneuvering of people and scenes to get laughs which sound more like titter. Such manipulation leads to the kind of laugh that comes from a gagline and not from something inherently funny in the situation."

Photoplay, May, 1942:
"The last picture made by Carole Lombard remains a fitting tribute to the vital, arresting beauty and personality of the star. There is no sense of shock at her posthumous appearance, so natural it seems that she should speak to us in this way."

Edgar Anstey,
The Spectator (London), May 8, 1942:
"Amongst our more solemn citizens, *To Be Or Not To Be* will become a touchstone of good taste: if you disapprove of it you will gain credit for a sense of the serious character of the war and of the sufferings of Nazi-occupied countries; if you find it the funniest comedy of the year, then you are very likely to be damned as

politically irresponsible. Fortunately my own estimate of the film qualifies me for neither category. Here is Ernst Lubitsch in something approaching his old form directing Carole Lombard, Jack Benny and a first-rate cast; and if the story happens to be a roaring farce set in the ruins of Warsaw, there is comfort in the fact that no Pole would ever identify his capital city with this beautiful, arc-softened debris. The comedy is good enough to survive the delicacy of the theme, but unfortunately *To Be Or Not To Be* is not all comedy. Messrs. Korda and Lubitsch have here and there abandoned their buffoonery to commiserate with the Poles and the Jews, and to make some return for their Hollywood comforts with sequences which they no doubt hope may prove to be anti-Nazi propaganda. At these points the film becomes very uncomfortable indeed. Once you have been persuaded to share a transatlantic vision of the Nazis as incompetent and rather lovable clowns, it is disturbing to be asked suddenly to share the producers' discovery that they are capable of doing quite a lot of damage. The story itself is a gargantuan essay in incredibility. It recounts the adventures of a conscientious but somewhat uninspired company of Polish actors who may be ham-like on the stage of their Warsaw theatre but become the completely convincing impersonators of their Nazi conquerors once their patriotic plots carry them to Gestapo head-quarters."

A Final Tribute to

Carole Lombard

She brought great joy to all who knew her and to millions who knew her only as a great artist. She gave unselfishly of time and talent to serve her government in peace and war. She loved her country. She is and always will be a star, one we shall never forget, nor cease to be grateful to.

—Franklin D. Roosevelt

Bibliography

Reviews and comments concerning Carole Lombard's appearance in motion pictures are listed by film title in italics. Other works pertaining to her personal and professional biography are cited by author.

Alpert, Hollis. *The Barrymores.* New York: Dial Press, 1964.

Arizona Kid, The (Review). *Motion Picture News,* May 23, 1930.

— — — . *The New York Times,* May 17, 1930, p. 21.

— — — . *The New York Times,* May 25, 1930, sec. 9, p. 5.

— — — . *Photoplay,* July, 1930.

Baldwin, Faith. "Do Hollywood Women Spoil Their Men?" *Photoplay,* May, 1939, pp. 18-19.

Baral, Robert. "Blonde Beauty Grows Up," *Photoplay,* May, 1939, pp. 34-35, 91.

Bentley, Janet. "She Gets Away With Murder," *Photoplay,* March, 1938, pp. 26, 88-89.

Biery, Ruth. "Why Carole Changed Her Mind," *Photoplay,* September, 1931, pp. 55-104-105.

Big News (Review). *Film Daily.* July 28, 1929, p. 8.

— — — . *The New York Times,* October 7, 1929, p. 22.

— — — . *Variety,* October 9, 1929.

Bolero (Review). *The New York Times,* February 17, 1934, p. 20.

Brief Moment (Review). *Motion Picture Herald,* October 7, 1933.

— — — . *The New York Times,* September 30, 1933, p. 18.

Bruce, Betsy. "The Camera-Shy Director," *Motion Picture Magazine,* September 1920, pp. 38-39, 104.

Busch, Noel F. "A Loud Cheer for the Screwball Girl," *Life,* October 17, 1938, pp. 48-51, 62-64.

Cannon, Robert C. *Van Dyke and the Mlthical City Hollywood.* Culver City: Murray and Gee, 1948.

Cheatham, Maude S. "The Dynamic Allan Dwan," *Motion Picture Magazine,* December, 1919, pp. 52-53.

Crichton, Kyle. "Fun in Flickers," *Colliers,* February 24, 1940, p. 11.

Crosby, Bing. *Call Me Lucky.* New York: Simon and Schuster, 1953.

Delehanty, Thornton. "Lubitsch Touch, Benny as Hamlet!" *New York Herald Tribune,* November 11, 1941.

Dickens, Homer. "Carole Lombard," *Films in Review,* February, 1961, pp. 70-86.

Doherty, Edward. "Can the Gable-Lombard Love Story Have a Happy Ending?" *Photoplay,* May, 1938, pp. 18-19, 77.

Dowling, Mark. "A New Way to Men's Hearts — As Told by Carole Lombard," *Motion Picture Magazine,* July, 1936, pp. 36, 82.

Dunphy, Christopher, et. al. *Handbook of General Information on the Paramount Pictures Production, Swing High, Swing Low.* Hollywood: Paramount Pictures, 1937.

Durgnat, Raymond. *The Crazy Mirror.* London: Faber, 1969.

Dwan, Allan. "The Prettiest Princess," *Photoplay,* September, 1924, pp. 66-67, 130.

Dynamite (Comment). *Photoplay,* March, 1929, p. 19.

Eagle and the Hawk (Review). *The New York Times,* May 13, 1933, p. 16.

— — — . *The New York Times,* May 21, 1933, sec. 9, p. 3.

Fast and Loose (Review). *The New York Times,* December 1, 1930, p. 21.

Fleming, William. "Perfect Abandon for Carole Lombard," *Shadowplay,* June, 1934, pp. 30-31, 64-66.

Fools for Scandal (Review). *The New York Times,* February 6, 1938, sec. 10, p. 5.

— — — . *The New York Times,* March 25, 1938, p. 15.

— — — . *Photoplay,* June, 1938.

From Hell to Heaven (Review). *The New York Times,* March 18, 1933, p. 9.

— — — . *The New York Times,* March 26, 1933, sec. 9, p. 3.

— — — . *Variety,* March 21, 1933.

Gargan, William. *Why Me? An Autobiography.* Garden City: Doubleday, 1969.

Garseau, Jean. *"Dear Mr. G —," The Biography of Clark Gable.* Boston and Toronto: Little, Brown, 1961.

Gassner, John and Dudley Nichols, editors. *Twenty Best Film Plays.* New York: Crown, 1943.

Gay Bride, The (Review). *The New York Times,* December 19, 1934, p. 27.

Hall, Gladys and Carole Lombard. "Why I Married Bill Powell," *Motion*

— — — . *Picture Magazine,* December, 1931, pp. 59, 99.

Hands Across the Table (Review). *The Times* (London), November 25, 1935, p. 10.

— — — . *New Republic,* November 13, 1935, p. 18.

Hastings, Dennison. "Clark Gable's Romantic Plight," *Photoplay,* September, 1936, pp. 12-13, 77.

Hayne, Donald, ed. *The Autobiography of Cecil B. deMille.* Englewood Cliffs: Prentice Hall, 1959.

Hays, Will H. *Memoirs.* Garden City: Doubleday, 1955.

Hearts and Spurs (Review). *Motion Picture News,* June 20, 1925, p. 3073.

High Voltage (Review). *Film Daily,* July 28, 1929, p. 9.

Holmes, John Clellon, "The Wonderful Movies of the 'Thirties," *Harper's,* December, 1965, pp. 51-55.

Hunt, Julie Lang. "How Carole Lombard Plans a Party," *Photoplay,* February, 1935, pp. 67-94.

I Take This Woman (Review). *The New York Times,* June 13, 1931, p. 20.

— — — . *The New York Times,* June 21, 1931, sec. 8, p. 3.

— — — . *Variety,* June 16, 1931.

It Pays to Advertise (Review). *The New York Times,* February 21, 1931, p. 15.

In Name Only (Review). *The New York Times,* August 4, 1939, p. 11.

― ― ― . *The Spectator* (London), December 8, 1939, p. 816.

― ― ― . *Time,* August 14, 1939.

Ladies' Man (Review). *Motion Picture Herald,* no date.

― ― ― . *The New York Times,* May 1, 1931, p. 30.

Lady by Choice (Review). *The New York Times,* November 17, 1934, p. 12.

― ― ― . *Variety,* November 20, 1934.

Lahue, Kalton C. *Continued Next Week, A History of the Moving Picture Serial.* Norman: University of Oklahoma, 1964.

Love Before Breakfast (Review). *Motion Picture Herald,* February 29, 1936, p. 41.

― ― ― . *The New York Times,* March 14, 1936, p. 10.

― ― ― . *Universal Weekly,* January 11, 1936, p. 24.

Marriage in Transit (Review). *Motion Picture News,* April 1, 1925, p. 1644.

Matchmaking Mamas (Review). *Motion Picture News,* March 30, 1929.

Me, Gangster (Review). *The New York Times,* October 22, 1928, p. 29.

― ― ― . *The New York Times,* October 28, 1928, sec. 9, p. 7.

― ― ― . *Variety,* October 28, 1928.

Mr. and Mrs. Smith (Review). *Hollywood Citizen News,* January 16, 1941.

― ― ― . *Hollywood Reporter,* January 16, 1941.

― ― ― . *New Republic,* March 4, 1941, p. 306.

― ― ― . *The Spectator* (London), April 4, 1941, p. 371.

My Man Godfrey (Review). *Commonweal,* August 24, 1936, p. 328.

― ― ― . *Motion Picture Herald,* June 20, 1936, p. 67.

― ― ― . *The New York Times,* Sept. 18, 1936, p. 18.

― ― ― . *The Spectator* (London), no date.

― ― ― . *The Times* (London), September 23, 1936, p. 10.

― ― ― . *Variety,* September 23, 1936, p. 16.

Ned McCobb's Daughter (Review). *Film Spectator* (Hollywood), Nov. 10, 1928, pp. 5-6.

― ― ― . *The New York Times,* February 18, 1929.

― ― ― . *The New York Times,* February 24, 1929, sec. 9, p. 7.

― ― ― . *Variety,* February 20, 1929.

No Man of Her Own (Review). *The New York Times,* December 31, 1932, p. 10.

No More Orchids (Review). *The New York Times,* January 2, 1933, p. 29.

― ― ― . *Variety,* November 18, 1932.

No One Man (Review). *Motion Picture Herald,* January 30, 1932, p. 45.

― ― ― . *The New York Times,* January 23, 1932, p. 18.

― ― ― . *Variety,* January 26, 1932.

Nothing Sacred (Review). *Life,* December 6, 1937, pp. 36-39.

― ― ― . *Motion Picture Herald,* August 21, 1937, pp. 16-17.

― ― ― . *Motion Picture Herald,* November 17, 1937, p. 52.

― ― ― . *The Nation,* December 18, 1937, p. 696.

― ― ― . *The New Statesman and Nation* (London), February 12, 1938, p. 248.

― ― ― . *The New York Times,* November 26, 1937, p. 27.

― ― ― . *The New York Times,* April 29, 1938, p. 6.

― ― ― . *The Spectator* (London), February 18, 1938, p. 271.

― ― ― . *Time,* December 6, 1937, pp. 49-50.

― ― ― . *Variety,* December 1, 1937.

Now and Forever (Review). *The New York Times,* October 13, 1934, p. 10.

― ― ― . *The New York Times,* October 14, 1934, sec. 10, p. 5.

O'Brien, Pat. *The Wind At My Back, The Life and Times of Pat O'Brien.* Garden City: Doubleday, 1964.

Officer O'Brien (Comment). *Motion Picture Herald,* July 6, 1929.

Patalas, Enno. *Stars, Geschichte der Filmidole.* Frankfurt am Main and Hamburg: Fischer Bücherei, 1967.

Perfect Crime, A (Review). *Motion Picture News,* March 5, 1921, p. 1859.
— — — . *Motion Picture News,* June 25, 1921, p. 118.
Power (Review). *Film Daily,* September 16, 1928, p. 13.
Princess Comes Across, The (Review). *Motion Picture Herald,* May 16, 1936,
    p. 29.
— — — . *The New York Times,* June 4, 1936, p. 27.
Pringle, Henry F. "Mr. and Mrs. Gable," *Ladies Home Journal,* May, 1940,
    p. 20.
Racketeer, The (Review). *Film Daily,* January 12, 1930, p. 12.
— — — . *The New York Times,* January 6, 1930, p. 30.
— — — . *Variety,* January 8, 1930.
Reid, James. "We Cover the Studios," *Photoplay,* March, 1938, pp. 55-5-, 87.
Rideout, Eric H. *The American Film.* London: Mitre Press, 1937.
Ritchie, Donald. *George Stevens. An American Romantic.* New York: Mu-
    seum of Modern Art, 1970.
Road to Glory (Review). *Bioscope* (London), April 1, 1926, p. 26.
— — — . *Moving Picture News,* February 20, 1926, p. 725.
— — — . *Variety,* April 28, 1926.
Rotha, Paul and Richard Griffith. *The Film Till Now, A Survey of World
    Cinema.* London: Spring Books, 1967.
Safety in Numbers (Review). *Motion Picture Herald,* June 7, 1930, p. 135.
— — — . *The New York Times,* May 31, 1930, p. 19.
— — — . *The New York Times,* June 8, 1930, sec. 9, p. 5.
Sennett, Mack and Cameron Ship. *The King of Comedy.* Garden City:
    Doubleday, 1954.
"No More Custard Pies," *Photoplay,* August, 1930, p. 10.
Seymore, Hart. "Carole Lombard Tells: 'How I Live By A Man's Code.'"
— — — . *Photoplay,* June, 1937, pp. 12-13, 78.
Show Folks (Review). *Motion Picture News,* December 15, 1928, p. 1815.
— — — . *Variety,* December 12, 1928.
Silke, James. "Man's Favorite Director, Howard Hawks," *Cinema* (Holly-
    wood), December, 1963, pp. 10-12, 31-32.
Sinners in the Sun (Review). *Motion Picture Herald,* May 21, 1932, p. 102.
— — — . *The New York Times,* May 14, 1932, p. 11.
— — — . *Variety,* May 17, 1932.
St. John, Adela Rogers. "A Gallant Lady . . . Carole Lombard," *Liberty,* Feb-
    ruary 28, 1942, pp. 21-24.
Supernatural, The (Review). *Motion Picture Herald,* April 29, 1933, p. 30.
— — — . *The New York Times,* April 22, 1933, p. 16.
Swing High, Swing Low (Review). *New Republic,* May 5, 1937, p. 386.
They Knew What They Wanted (Review). *Commonweal,* October 25, 1940,
    p. 25.
— — — . *Life,* September 30, 1940, pp. 47-50.
— — — . *The New York Times,* October 11, 1940, p. 25.
— — — . *Spectator* (London), January 10, 1941, p. 35.
— — — . *Theatre Arts,* December, 1940, pp. 869-870.
Thomaier, William. "Early Sound Comedy," *Films in Review,* May, 1958,
    pp. 254-262.
Thorp, Margaret. *America at the Movies,* New Haven: Yale University, 1939.
To Be or Not to Be (Review). *Commonweal,* March 13, 1942, p. 513.
— — — . *Movie-Radio Guide,* February 14-20, 1942, pp. 2-3.
— — — . *National Board of Review,* Spring, 1942.
— — — . *New Republic,* March 23, 1942, p. 399.
— — — . *The New York Times,* March 22, 1942.
— — — . *The New York Times,* March 29, 1942.
— — — . *Spectator* (London), May 8, 1942, p. 442.
True Confession (Review). *Atlantic Monthly,* May 6, 1938, p. 238.
— — — . *The New York Times,* December 16, 1937, p. 35.

— — — . *The Spectator* (London), December 31, 1937, p. 1177.

— — — . *The Times* (London), December 20, 1937, p. 10.

Truffaut, Francois. *Hitchcock.* New York: Simon and Schuster, 1967.

Turconi, Davide. *Mack Sennett, il "re delle comiche."* Rome: Edizioni dell'Ateneo, 1961.

Twentieth Century (Review). *Motion Picture Herald,* April 21, 1934, p. 35.

— — — . *The New York Times,* May 4, 1934, p. 24.

— — — . *The New York Times,* May 13, 1934, sec. 9, p. 2.

— — — . *The Times* (London), July 9, 1934, p. 12.

— — — . *Variety,* May 8, 1934.

Up Pops the Devil (Review), *International Photographer,* June, 1931, pp. 39-40.

— — — . *The New York Times,* May 16, 1931, p. 13.

— — — . *The New York Times,* May 24, 1931, sec. 8, p. 5.

— — — . *Variety,* May 20, 1931.

Vigil in the Night (Review). *Commonweal,* March 15, 1940, p. 456.

— — — . *Film Daily,* February 23, 1940, p. 5.

— — — . *Motion Picture Herald,* February 10, 1940, pp. 36, 38.

— — — . *The New York Times,* March 9, 1940, p. 19.

— — — . *New Yorker,* March 9, 1940, p. 85.

— — — . *Time,* March 11, 1940, p. 82.

Virtue (Review). *Motion Picture Herald,* November 5, 1932, p. 44.

— — — . *The New York Times,* October 25, 1932, p. 24.

We're Not Dressing (Review). *Literary Digest,* May 12, 1934, p. 34.

— — — . *The New York Times,* April 26, 1934, p. 27.

— — — . *Newsweek,* May 12, 1934.

White Woman (Review). *Daily Variety,* October 14, 1933.

— — — . *The New York Times,* December 3, 1933, sec. 9, p. 9.

— — — . *Variety,* November 21, 1933.